1982

SOLVING PROBLEMS KIDS CARE ABOUT

OTHER GOODYEAR BOOKS IN SCIENCE, MATH, & SOCIAL STUDIES

For information about these, or Goodyear books in Language Arts, Reading,
General Methods, and Centers, write to
JANET JACKSON
Goodyear Publishing Company
1640 Fifth Street
Santa Monica, CA 90401
(213) 393-6731

Solving Problems
Kids
Care About

RANDALL J. SOUVINEY

University of California, San Diego

Goodyear Publishing Company

Santa Monica, California

Library of Congress Cataloging in Publication Data

SOUVINEY, RANDALL.
    Solving problems kids care about.

    Bibliography
    1. Problem solving, Group—Study and teaching.
2. Activity programs in education. 3. Problem
solving—Study and teaching. I. Title.
HM133.S8   153.4'3   81–509
ISBN 0–8302–8653–5   AACR2

For my mother and father . . .
Who had the courage to give me the
freedom I needed as a child.

Text of "Homemade Boat," "Invention,"
"Smart," and "Stone Telling" from *Where the Sidewalk Ends:
The Poems of Shel Silverstein,* copyright © 1974,
by Shel Silverstein. By permission
of Harper & Row, Publishers, Inc.

Current printing (last number):

10 9 8 7 6 5 4 3 2 1
ISBN: 0–8302–8653–5
Y–8653–1

Printed in the United States of America.

CONTENTS

153.43
8729

102,083

HOW TO USE THIS BOOK

HOMEMADE BOAT

This boat that we just built is just fine —
And don't try to tell us it's not.
The sides and the back are divine —
It's the bottom I guess we forgot . . . . . .

SHEL SILVERSTEIN
(From *Where the Sidewalk Ends*)

You do not need to be an expert problem solver to teach effective problem solving skills. Our primary role as teachers is to establish a nonthreatening environment to encourage efficient problem-solving behaviors among our students. We must also have the courage to learn along with our students, since many of these important problem-solving skills may be as new to us as to our classes.

Here are few hints which you may find helpful:

1. Scan through section I (especially chapter 2) to review strategies and techniques for teaching mathematical problem solving. In particular, look at:

   a. Problems Worth Solving
   b. The Four-Step Problem Solving Plan
   c. Strategies for Problem Solving

2. Think about how to organize your classroom to foster effective problem-solving sessions. The following sequence is suggested:

   a. Begin with the whole class problem-solving warm-up activities to encourage divergent thinking and cooperative problem solving behaviour.
   b. Discuss each particular strategy in a large group (for example, *working backwards*). Break up into groups-of-four and assign everyone the same problem (perhaps *"Stack the Deck"*).
   c. Introduce each strategy in this way, allowing ample time for a whole-class discussion after each session to encourage a sharing of strategies and solutions.
   d. As you and your students become more adept at using various solution strategies, offer a choice of problems. Always allow time for discussion.

3. Other recommendations:

   a. Initial problem-solving sessions should be brief. Extend the duration with experience.
   b. Try to schedule sessions frequently, at least twice a week.
   c. Initially, plan a whole class discussion after each session. Later, these large group discussions may be required less frequently.

d. Every child (group) may be unable to completely solve every problem in the time available. The problems are designed, however, so that everyone is encouraged to make some progress and offer input during the discussions.

e. The Problem-Starter sheets should be reproduced for each child. The hints provided should help individuals (or groups) formulate a solution strategy.

f. The problems are sequenced so that they become increasingly complex. With sufficient experience, intermediate and junior-high level students should be successful in solving most of the problems, while the more complex examples may be inappropriate for younger children.

g. After working through the problems of interest in this book, perhaps you and your class might enjoy enlarging your collection by reviewing the sources in the bibliography or asking people in your community. Keep in mind the selection criteria when choosing your "problems worth solving."

INTRODUCTION

STONE TELLING

How do we tell if a window is open?
Just throw a stone at it.
Does it make a noise?
It doesn't?
Well, it was open.
Now let's try another . . .
CRASH!
It wasn't!
    SHEL SILVERSTEIN
    (From *Where the Sidewalk Ends*)

This book was written for people who want to become more successful problem solvers. It is specifically designed to be used as a sourcebook of ideas and activities by elementary and junior-high school teachers. Though the problems are couched in situations chosen to pique the imagination of young minds, adults should find most of the problems intellectually stimulating. In fact, we have uncovered distressingly few problems found boring by adults that children do not find to be as well. Regretfully, the opposite doesn't necessarily hold either.

Section I provides a summary of background notes and strategies for teaching mathematical problem solving. A general solving plan is presented along with suggestions for establishing an effective classroom environment. The remainder of the book is devoted to the presentation of over thirty carefully selected problems ready for immediate classroom use. A discussion of each problem is provided along with a detailèd solution and reproducible student Problem-Starter sheet. Solutions are included primarily as background information for teachers. It is not intended that students be limited to the described solution strategy or, in many cases, the answer provided. On the contrary, the problems were specifically selected to be susceptible to multiple solution strategies and may in several cases have a range of acceptable answers.

We were careful to avoid including problems with "tricky" or "cutsie" solutions. For example, you won't find problems like the one that follows:

A little league team had numbered shirts as below. The catcher (#6) was late for practice. While they were waiting, the coach decided to give the team a little mental exercise. He told them to divide themselves into two groups of four so that the total of their jersey numbers for each group would be equal.

The team quickly figured out that the problem couldn't be solved since the total of all their jersey numbers was odd (39). The shortstop (#9) finally solved the problem by standing on her head! There are exactly four ways to break into two "equal" groups of four if the 9 turns into a 6.

1,2,7,8, and 5,3,4,6

1,4,5,8, and 2,3,6,7

1,3,6,8, and 2,4,5,7

1,4,6,7, and 2,3,5,8

We find that problems of this type tend to frustrate and offend novice problem solvers. Such problems encourage the unproductive strategy of initially looking for a clever trick or a slight-of-hand instead of working toward a deeper understanding of the problem situation. We suggest such problems be reserved for informal social gatherings and not be included in the serious business of developing effective problem-solving strategies.

Many individuals contributed to the development and production of *Solving Problems Kids Care About*. Most of the ideas presented are not original but rather adapt and extend the thoughts and experiences of several respected colleagues: most notably George Polya, Martin Gardiner, Carol Greenes, and Marilyn Burns. In addition I would like to thank Joan Akers and John Wavrik for their many helpful suggestions and criticisms during the planning of the manuscript. Also, without the invaluable support and encouragement from Chris Jennison and the Goodyear Publishing people, the project might never have been completed. I wish to thank Kiri Mimi for his original illustrations and Gail Anders, Lauyang Posanau and Priscilla Warbat for their tireless efforts in preparing the final draft for publication. Finally, I offer my deepest appreciation to my wife, Barbara, for trying to make sense out of my original henscratches, for her perceptive advice concerning the classroom activities, and especially for her patient support throughout our travels as these pages were taking shape.

R. J. S.
Papua New Guinea
January, 1981

Teaching Strategies for Mathematical Problem Solving

CHAPTER 1

WHAT'S WORTH KNOWING

SMART

My dad gave me one dollar bill
'Cause I'm his smartest son,
And I swapped it for two shiny quarters
'Cause two is more than one!

And then I took the quarters
And traded them to Lou
For three dimes—I guess he don't know
That three is more than two!

Just then, along came old blind Bates
And just 'cause he can't see
He gave me four nickels for my three dimes,
And four is more than three!

And I took the nickels to Hiram Coombs
Down at the seed-feed store,
And the fool gave me five pennies for them,
And five is more than four!

And then I went and showed my dad,
And he got red in the cheeks
And closed his eyes and shook his head—
Too proud of me to speak!

SHEL SILVERSTEIN
(from *Where the Sidewalk Ends*)

As our world changes before our eyes—our knowledge base becoming obsolete at an alarming rate and value systems seeming to change with or without us—what do we teach our children who must survive and prosper in a changing environment we may scarcely be able to imagine? What is worth teaching today that will be worth knowing in the year 2000?

Two educational issues come to mind which hold the greatest promise for helping children become independent, competent actors in their world. First, in virtually every field, accepted practices are becoming obsolete as rapidly as new knowledge develops. For example, in teaching it becomes more and more difficult to remain current as the years pass. Teachers must search for the essential strands which transcend the blizzard of competing ideologies and techniques in order to function effectively in their classrooms. Specialization, the traditional mechanism designed to contend with information explosion, will continue to flourish. The time is long past when one individual possessed a thorough understanding of an entire field. (Karl Gauss is purported to be the last individual to understand all contemporary mathematics, and he died over one hundred years ago. We have developed more mathematics in the past twenty years than in the thousands of years before Gauss!)

Clearly, we must look at learning differently if the children in our elementary schools today are to gain a sense of competence in their lives tomorrow. Facts and relationships between facts will become less important, learned temporarily and later replaced by a new set of relevant facts and relationships. We are discovering that many of the "facts" associated with everyday life are reflections of our own values and may not be valid in other societies. Ethnocentric thinking, though comfortable, will be less useful in our shrinking, multicultural world.

A knowledge of mathematics will be increasingly important in tomorrow's world, although certain elements will be more useful than others. Computation will continue to play an important role; however, we will depend more and more on the speed and accuracy of the calculator for large computations. The ability to understand and solve naturally occurring problems will be a prized attribute. Facts are important only insofar as they provide a medium for understanding a particular problem; creative solution strategies, once developed, remain useful when confronting a wide range of situations. There is little value to methodically deriving the wrong answer to ten decimal places.

A second challenge to the education community (which may have even greater impact on what is worth knowing) is the availability of versatile low-cost personal computers. These crafty little devices are truly technological marvels, unheard of only a few years ago. The machine that sits on my desk while I'm writing this introduction cost less than $1500 and is more powerful than the computer that served the entire university only twelve years ago, valued at several million dollars. If development continues over the next five years, a machine one-thousand times more powerful will be available for under $500. Millions of these personal computing devices will be challenging and entertaining people by the mid-1980s.

The education community cannot afford to ignore the impact such devices will have on learning and curriculum design. Access to vast stores of factual information (history, literature, sports statistics, election results, geographic facts, languages, etc.) will depend on how well individuals "communicate" with their computers. We may soon see the day when you can ask your personal computer to argue with your bank's computer to resolve disputes in your checking account. The microcomputer promises to convert our most popular spectator sport, watching television, into a highly stimulating interactive activity. The ultimate effect on our society as a whole is sure to be at least as significant as the introduction of the printing press or the onset of the industrial revolution.

What does this mean for elementary education today? Learning to compute will remain an important part of the math curriculum; however, conceptual understanding and estimation skills will take precedence over accuracy and speed with large computations. Use of ratio fractions will diminish in favor of early introduction of decimals. Computing devices (calculators, special purpose devices, microcomputers) will be utilized in increasing numbers at all levels of education. If used properly, these machines will become a vital factor in our efforts to enhance the ability of our students to solve mathematical problems in school and throughout their lives.

PROBLEMS WORTH SOLVING

Before turning our attention to specific problem-solving teaching strategies, we must discuss the characteristics of problem situations appropriate for novice problem solvers. (Here, novice refers to level of experience, which may have little to do with one's age.) Our goal is to provide classroom experiences which encourage divergent and logical thinking by our students; consider the following criteria for problem selection.

An ideal problem situation should

1. be readily understandable to the student, yet the solution should not be immediately apparent;
2. be intrinsically motivating and intellectually stimulating;
3. have more than one solution "path";
4. require only previously learned arithmetic operations and concepts;
5. lend itself to being solved over a reasonable period of time (not a simple computational procedure);
6. be somewhat open-ended (solutions should suggest new problems);
7. integrate various subject areas—mathematics, science, social studies, fine arts;
8. be well enough defined so you will know when it's solved.

Convergent and Divergent Problems

These eight criteria do not characterize the type of problems found in elementary textbooks. Word problems are generally presented in a *convergent* manner whereby the student decides which operation(s) to apply to the values provided, in order to determine the correct answer. This type of presentation offers a rather restricted view of problem solving.

Though many problems encountered in life involve quantities (counting, measures, money), rarely are these values presented in an organized, symbolic form. An individual first must recognize that a problem exists and be motivated to seek understanding. This initial, seemingly aimless, trial-and-error stage of problem solving generally includes doodling, sketching, estimating, measuring, counting, asking questions and listening. With children it is especially important to encourage the exploration of ideas and concrete materials to define problem parameters and eventual solution strategies. Most of all, such problems offer children a glimpse of the creative act which teachers, engineers, accountants, mothers, politicians, architects and scientists are engaged in daily—namely, the dissecting (analysis) of complex events and the piecing together (synthesis) of familiar elements to derive order and meaning from novel problem situations. The following example illustrates the type of divergent problem situation which is easy to describe yet requires a bit of "messing about" with ideas and sketches to fully define the problem situation and predict an appropriate solution strategy.

Billiard Table Math

Suppose you have a rectangular billiard table like the one below. If you shoot out from the lower left corner at 45° (split the corner square), which corner will the ball end up in?

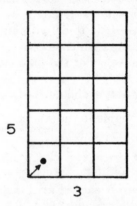

First, it is not at all clear that the ball will end up in any corner. Also, you have to realize that a billiard ball bounces off at the same angle it strikes the cushion (45° in this case). It might require a bit of experimenting to justify this *one* element of the problem. One convenient way to test your skill is to sketch the table on 1 cm graph paper and trace the path of the ball.

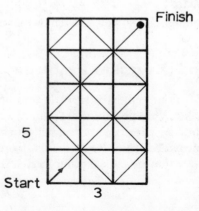

This odd-sized table (conventional size is 3 × 6) provides an "interesting" game, finishing in the upper right corner. Notice that the ball crosses every square. Is this true for other sized rectangular tables? Will the ball always end in a corner (assume the dimensions are whole units)? Can you predict which corner the ball will end in, without tracing its path? (To keep things simple, remember to shoot out from the lower left corner at 45°.)

Each of these questions is easy to understand, but the solution is not immediately apparent. The solution to the initial problem raises several new and interesting questions. The intellectual and motor skills necessary to effectively participate in this problem should be available to most children age nine or older. The situation is motivating and intellectually stimulating to most kids. It's reasonably easy to determine when you have solved the problem. Based on our problem selection criteria, this problem seems to be an ideal candidate for classroom use.

Let's continue our game. One strategy is to try out tables of various sizes and see if any useful insight is gained from the results or if a pattern emerges. This state of experimentation not only allows the collection of potentially useful data, but also encourages a high level of involvement on the part of the solver. As we will discuss later, motivation and mind set play a significant role in effective problem solving.

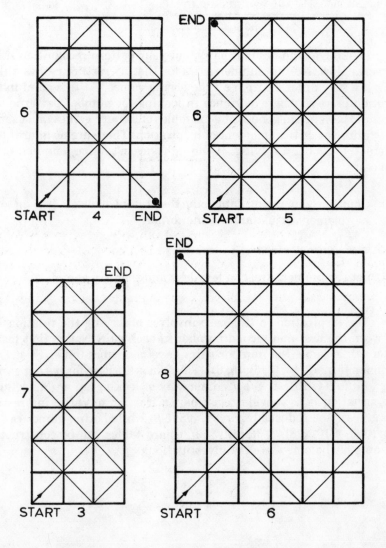

"Interesting" or "Boring" Game.   Do table dimensions determine if a game is *interesting* (every square crossed by the ball) or *boring* (some squares not crossed)? Perhaps a table would help organize the data we collected. Using graph paper, check out the data in the following table. Play a few additional games and enter those data as well. The first number of each pair represents the length of the base of the table (horizontal axis) and the second number represents the height (vertical axis).

Billiard Games

Interesting	Boring
(3, 5)	(4, 6)
(5, 6)	(6, 8)
(3, 7)	(4, 10)
(4, 9)	(3, 9)
(5, 4)	(4, 4)
(,)	(,)
(,)	(,)

Looking at the number pairs, put your pattern recognition skills to work. How are the number pairs for the interesting games alike? How are they different from all the boring games? At this point in the solution process, past experience in looking for number patterns and recent experience in generating examples of billiard games must somehow foster the critical moment of inspiration. There are no guarantees in creative problem solving. If the light doesn't shine, one has three choices:

1. Continue generating data using the present strategy, hoping some key element is just around the corner;

2. Try a new strategy;

3. Let the problem "rest" a few days and then try again.

The inspiration in this case involves observing the relationship between the first and second number in each pair. Notice that for an interesting game, the number pairs have no factors (other than 1) in common [e.g., (3, 7), (3, 5), (5, 6)]. This is not the case for boring games [e.g., (4, 6), (4, 10), (6, 8)]. Another way of looking at, or "modeling," the situation is to consider each pair a fraction or ratio. Interesting games can't be reduced (e.g., 3/7, 3/5, 5/6) while boring games can be (e.g., 4/6, 4/10, 6/8). A "family" of billiard tables can be constructed, opening a whole new area of investigation.

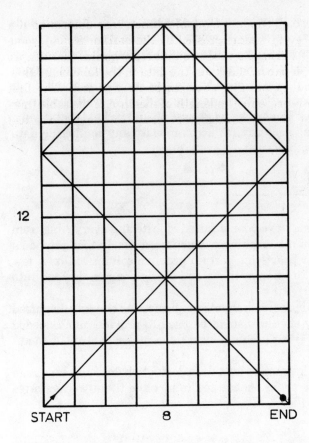

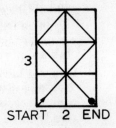

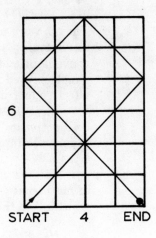

Notice the similar pattern the ball makes for each game in the (2, 3) family. Is this true for other families [e.g., (3, 4), (6, 8), (9, 12)]? Will the ball end up in the same corner for every game in a family? Will this information help us predict which corner the ball will end up in for all games? Completing a table like the one below and collecting data on interesting games only should make the situation more transparent. (If you have done your homework, you should have found that every *boring* game has an *interesting* family member that ends in the same corner.)

The Ball Stops Here

Lower Left	Upper Left	Upper Right	Lower Right
	(3, 4)	(3, 7)	(4, 5)
	(5, 6)	(5, 9)	(6, 7)
	(7, 8)	(5, 7)	(4, 9)
	(,)	(,)	(,)

Again, recognizing a pattern that distinguishes among the columns should inspire an "ah-ha" experience. A simple way to describe the solution is that, for an interesting game, the ball always stops at the end of the even axis. If there is no even axis [e.g., (5, 7)], the ball ends in the upper right hand corner. (It never returns to its starting point.)

The last step in the process is to convince yourself that your solution is true for all cases. Generally, it is not necessary to construct a formal proof at this level. Unless it is a life and death situation or you're risking the family fortune, working out a few well chosen examples should suffice. This "proof by desire" should be held tentatively, ready to be altered as necessary to accommodate any conflicting data that might arise in subsequent experiments.

Word Problems

Though word problems have been accused of fostering everything from math anxiety to premature baldness, when used wisely they provide a convenient means for practicing certain problem solving skills. A few simple procedures can change those end-of-the-chapter demons into effective learning activities.

First of all, word problems should not be used as cleverly disguised drill activities. They should instead be used to provide much needed experience in deciphering problem situations under controlled conditions.

To give children practice translating English into the language of mathematics, give them "headlines" and have them write stories which fill in the details.

Headline: *2 × 12 = 24*

Students in Ms. Miller's class decided to take pictures of all the teachers in the school. They earned enough money for two rolls of film with 12 pictures on each roll. They can take 24 pictures in all.

Experience with headlines helps children convert mathematical sentences into realistic dialogue. The opposite procedure is also useful. Have students write an appropriate headline for problems found in their texts. It is not necessary for them to compute solutions in order to write headlines. Avoiding the actual computations allows children to concentrate on deciphering the problem situation and devising a solutional plan. A calculator can be useful at this stage as well. For example, a possible headline for the problem below might be: *"12 ÷ 4 = 3 omelets."*

Problem: If four people decide to share equally a dozen eggs for breakfast, how many will each person get?

Textbook word problems are carefully chosen to be convergent—that is, they require a limited number of steps which lead to one "correct" answer. Though such problems are convenient, the solution strategies they require generally involve recognizing when to apply an appropriate rule—the most difficult strategy for beginners. Any analysis of the problem is generally quite limited, while the synthesis of appropriate computations comprises most of the solution effort.

Problems which involve conducting an experiment, organizing data or observing a pattern should become part of your classroom's daily mathematical diet. You will find many problems of this type included in the following sections, as well as in the references listed in the bibliography. Using word problem activities such as headlines provides practice with English-to-mathematics translations. However, these activities should be mixed with more divergent problems to encourage the development of analytical problem-solving skills. Remember, problems encountered in the real world are almost never presented in written form. It is through the process of defining and understanding the problem situation and its conditions that the seeds of solution are sown.

A Word About "Real World" Problems

Problems found in math books (including this one) generally differ from real world problems in two important ways, and the success you and your students enjoy when applying the techniques discussed here and in the next chapter to practical problems encountered in daily life will depend greatly on your ability to understand and compensate for these distinctions.

First, some problems in everyday life may have *no* solution under the naturally occurring conditions. Remember those carefully stated conditions found in most "school" problems: you can remove one marble at a time, return it to the bag and shake. The implicit conditions are also relatively transparent: don't look up the answer in the back of the book! With real world problems the conditions, both stated and implicit, become far more important.

For example, consider the impending world oil crisis. Prior to 1970, most people realized that petroleum supplies were limited and were rapidly being depleted by an energy-hungry world. The problem for the United States became one of meeting the growing energy demand of industry and the public. Several "solutions" were suggested including conservation, increasing efforts to find new domestic oil fields, synthetic fuels, higher import quotas and alternative energy sources. The easiest solution, increasing import quotas, is no longer working. The problem remains the same but the *conditions* have changed. The complex Mideast situation has seriously affected sales of crude. Atomic power is under fire. Long and troubled waits in gas lines have become commonplace. Many people can not afford to heat their homes during the winter.

Real world problems are rarely solved permanently. When trouble arises, *new* solutions must be found to meet *new* conditions. Strategies originally considered and discarded may now take on new promise. For example, synthetic fuels made from plentiful coal and shale were once too expensive to make. Now they are viable alternatives, since gasoline is selling at well over one dollar a gallon. Success with such problems is as much due to an ability to adapt to explicit conditions as it is to understanding the processes of analysis and synthesis.

The second distinction between "school" problems and "folk" problems involves the underlying value structure of the solver. If the solution to a problem is persistently elusive, *always* check your assumptions. Though this advice is generally sound, when a values conflict is suspected it is absolutely essential.

A values conflict occurs when two individuals experience the same event and arrive at two opposing points of view and, based on their own value systems, each of the points of view is absolutely correct. When this occurs, a solution to the conflict may be impossible unless one or both sets of values are compromised. Values conflicts occur between age groups, political parties, socio-economic groups and especially in multicultural environments.

These practical social problems, which many times show up in classrooms, at customer-relations desks at department stores, and in the international political arena, are often exasperatingly difficult to solve. One common pitfall is failing to recognize that a values conflict is at the heart of the problem in the first place—the solver *assumes* everyone involved in the situation has a common understanding of the events. Solutions to "real world" problems often require a deep understanding of each other's value system, considerable mutual respect, and an overall balance of power. Violating these conditions often invites a micro-war in the classroom or a real war if sufficient national interest is at stake.

The techniques described in this book are useful in solving an interesting though necessarily limited class of problems. In the real world such methods certainly contribute to the solution of practical problems but are not sufficient in themselves to unravel the complexities of human interaction.

TWO TYPES OF REASONING

Regressive and progressive reasoning are two characteristic views of *creative problem solving* (the solution of novel problems). Both were originally described by the Greeks and have been subsequently refined through two thousand years by countless mathematicians and scientists. Regressive and progressive reasoning have complementary features which, when applied appropriately, aid greatly in planning and implementing a solution strategy (see Figure 1).

Analysis (regressive reasoning) is logically working through a problem backwards. Beginning with a well-defined (though not completely understood) problem situation, the solver searches for a simpler condition which, if true, will guarantee the solution of the original situation. Analysis continually reduces the complexity of a situation until the interrelationships between the preconditions of the problem become clear. For example, if you found yourself stranded miles from the nearest gas station because a prankster let the air out of your bicycle tire, a simple precondition which guarantees you will be back on the road is to somehow refill your tire. By continuing the process of deducing appropriate preconditions, you eventually arrive at a condition that can be easily satisfied—perhaps turning the bicycle upside down and temporarily filling the tire with water. Your analysis should lead directly to a plan which can then be carried out by repeating the steps in the opposite direction (simplest to most complex). This complementary process is called *synthesis* (progressive reasoning). Any inadvertent error in logic made during the analytical phase will be graphically discovered during the implementation of the solution plan—it may take all night to fill the tire with water!

Most problems require the coordinated application of both process-es, though as problems become more routine, less analysis may be needed.

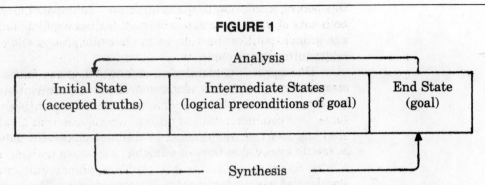

FIGURE 1

Analysis

| Initial State (accepted truths) | Intermediate States (logical preconditions of goal) | End State (goal) |

Synthesis

Analysis

Analysis is the process of simplifying a currently obscure situation by initially assuming the goal is true and applying known logical opera-tions to establish a set of logical preconditions, subsequently arriving at a known or transparent state. The primary distinction between analysis and synthesis is that with analysis all the information necessary to solve the problem situation is embodied in the goal statement, though it may be initially obscure and unintelligible. Analysis continually reduces the complexity of the situation until the interrelationships become clear. Carefully describing the problem goal is vital if a successful solution is to be found. Chess players, lawyers, doctors and detectives rely heavily on analysis for their problem solving needs.

Synthesis

Synthesis is the process of applying known processes (from a wide range of possible processes) to given factual information (initial state) in order to attain a specific goal (end state). As the initial state is adapted by each process, the relationship between the current state and the desired goal is evaluated and subsequent processes applied in order to eventually reduce the misfit between the goal and the current state to zero. Many unique solution paths may be possible for such problems. Learning to ride a bicycle or build a model airplane are examples of synthetic solu-tions.

Ends-Means Analysis

An alternative way of thinking about these reciprocal methods of rea-soning is a process called *ends-means analysis. Ends* refers to a clear statement of the goal or intent. The better the "ends" are described for a given problem, the easier the solution. The *means* consist of a set of known concepts and principles which can be brought to bear on the given situation.

The first step when applying ends-means analysis is to state your goal clearly so you will know when you have solved the problem. In many cases, this initial step requires a good deal of thought and ex-perimentation. The results of your efforts, however, will be well worth the trouble.

Once a clear goal has been established, the next step is to determine a sequence of actions which, if carried out, will insure a satisfactory solution (analysis). Finally, as each step in the solution process is carried out (synthesis), the current state of the situation is examined and compared to the desired result. If the degree of misfit has diminished, the plan is continued. If not, the problem and solution plan are reexamined. Ends-means analysis embodies the *analysis* of the problem situation, the development of a sequence of actions, and a scheme for monitoring the *syntheses* of these actions as you work towards a solution.

Structured Problem Solving

An additional way to view the problem solving process is borrowed from the field of computer science. The first step in structured problem solving is to establish a well-defined goal. Using analysis, a "tree" of subgoals which are preconditions for the desired result is determined. This "chunking" process is continued with each subgoal until all the individual tasks are well known (primitive). Finally, through synthesis, the process is reversed; individual subgoals are accomplished and coordinated with each other. If the process is successful, the original need will be satisfied. If not, the goal must be reviewed in light of the error and analysis resumed anew.

As the low-level chunks and their uses become more familiar to the user, less analysis may be required. When a set of related chunks becomes completely generalized, a whole class of problems can be addressed by relying on a synthesis of these well known chunks. For example, in attempting to design a ship's hull which will be very stable in rough seas, a novice might have to build several models before discovering the optimum combination of length, width, depth and shape (analysis). An experienced builder draws upon a well-coordinated set of skills (chunks) which allow him to confidently predict hull performance characteristics (synthesis).

Our sample tree diagram provides a practical example of planning a backpacking trip. Many implicit conditions apply to the problem of going backpacking. Each situation is unique. The solution below is but one example of the key considerations which might be taken into account when planning a trip. The primitive chunks (lowest-level tasks on each branch) must be coordinated in order to synthesize a solution. For example, if money isn't obtained prior to going to the store, embarrassment may ensue. It is possible to make the solution more elegant (efficient) if, for example, all the trips to the store are combined in one journey. It is interesting to note that the set of primitive (known) chunks which solve a particular problem may not be unique. Their order as well as their content may vary.

Regardless of what convenient structure we use to explain creative problem solving, an intangible element remains which defies rigorous description yet seems fundamental to the entire enterprise. Factual knowledge and past problem-solving experience are certainly important; however, an element of chance pervades any novel problem situation. An effective problem solver must not only possess appropriate skills and knowledge to bring to bear on the situation, but he or she must also have the motivation, persistence and self-confidence to

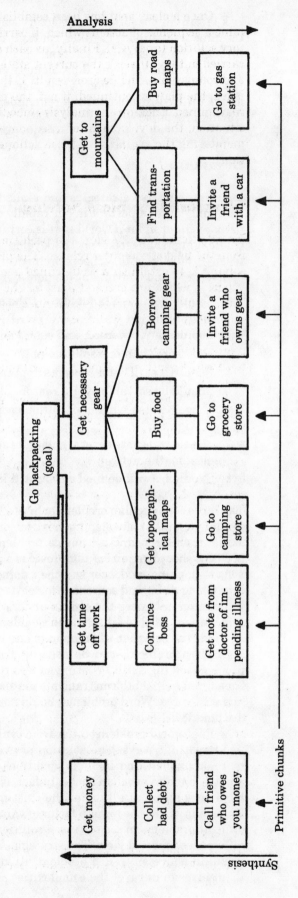

Structured Problem Solving Tree

Analysis

Synthesis

Primitive chunks

risk failure in pursuing a satisfactory solution. Though "chance favors the prepared mind," it takes courage to see a truly novel problem through to a satisfactory solution.

An additional general problem solving plan is described in Chapter 2. The original version of this plan was described by George Polya and is utilized throughout the remainder of this book as the means of solving problems.

Summary

Learning effective strategies and skills for solving novel problems is becoming more important in our rapidly changing world. Schools must prepare children for a world that is certain to be far more complex and challenging than today's. To develop such problem-solving skills, teachers must carefully choose problem situations which offer a balance of divergent and convergent elements. A problem worth solving—

1. Should be understandable, yet the solution should not be readily apparent;
2. Should be motivating and easy to describe;
3. Has more than one solution path;
4. Requires skills and concepts appropriate for the grade level;
5. Should be solvable over a reasonable time period;
6. Is open ended whereby solutions suggest new questions to be investigated;
7. Should integrate several subject areas (science, social studies, fine arts, mathematics);
8. Should be well defined so you will know when it's solved.

The more a particular problem exhibits these criteria, the greater potential it has for developing healthy problem-solving attitudes and skills in children and all novice problem solvers. In general, a good problem should require a high level of involvement on the part of the solver—making models or sketches, doing experiments, collecting and organizing data, and searching for patterns and generalizations. Such interaction enhances the child's understanding of the problem situation, generates clues that weren't evident in the problem description, and aids the selection of an appropriate solution strategy.

Word problems can be used as a means for practicing various problem-solving skills. Writing stories to describe a number sentence "headline" helps children translate mathematics into everyday English and vice-versa. Word problems should not be used as cleverly disguised arithmetic drills.

Real world problems differ from typical mathematics problems in two important ways. The solution of everyday problems depends far more on explicit and implicit conditions than do the well defined examples found in problem books. In fact, many real world problems may have no solution at all under the existing conditions. The second distinction involves the human factor of values conflicts. Many of the most difficult problems in society resist solution because of these underlying differences in world view. The strategies described in this book may be useful in addressing such problem situations but are not sufficient in themselves to unravel the complexities of human interaction.

Mathematical problem solving depends on two basic types of reasoning:

1. analysis or regressive reasoning
2. synthesis or progressive reasoning.

Knowledge of these two processes is fundamental to understanding general problem-solving plans such as *ends-means analysis* and *structured problem solving*. Ends-means analysis and structured problem solving both involve the analysis of a problem situation as a set of well-defined actions and the synthesis of these actions as you work towards a solution.

Ends-means analysis refers to a process of carefully describing a desired result (end) and determining a sequence of actions (means) which seem to insure a satisfactory solution. Subsequently, when carrying out each step in the solution process, the current status is compared to the desired result in order to monitor progress and make appropriate adjustments in the solution.

Structured problem solving is a process of constructing a "tree" of subgoals (chunks) which together form a complete set of preconditions for the desired result. These subgoals are further subdivided until they reach a "primitive" or known state. Reversing the process completes the solution.

CHAPTER 2

IN SEARCH OF SOLUTIONS

INVENTION

I've done it, I've done it!
Guess what I've done!
Invented a light that plugs into the sun.
The sun is bright enough,
The bulb is strong enough,
But, oh, there's only one thing wrong . . .

The cord ain't long enough.

SHEL SILVERSTEIN
(from *Where the Sidewalk Ends)*

No single solution strategy is sufficient for all problems. Successful problem solvers may have to bring several strategies to bear on particularly novel problems before a moment of inspiration finally makes the situation transparent. Each strategy can only serve to increase your understanding of the problem and its conditions, enhancing the probability that some obscure relationship will become apparent. Through this initial process of investigation and discovery, a seemingly novel problem may turn out to be related to a previously solved problem and therefore be subject to a similar solution.

Several general problem-solving plans have been developed over the past two thousand years to assist individuals in their assaults on the novel or unknown. Pappus (circa 300 A.D.) offers one of the earliest descriptions of a formal analytic problem-solving model. One general problem-solving model relatively accessible to elementary-aged children is described by George Polya in his most readable work, *How to Solve It* (Princeton University Press, 1973). Polya's general problem-solving "heuristic" is easily understood and is applicable to a wide range of mathematical and practical problems. This four-step plan helps novices of all ages organize the entire solution enterprise, thereby significantly increasing the probability of success in solving unique problems.

It is often beneficial for small groups of two to four children to work together on a common problem. Though most schooling stresses the cognitive and affective development of the *individual,* practically every major scientific engineering problem solved in the past century succumbed to a team effort. In light of this fact it seems appropriate that we begin developing these interactional problem-solving skills at an early age. Brainstorming, discussion skills, data gathering, subdividing the work load, and group decision making all constitute effective group problem solving strategies.

GROUPS-OF-FOUR

One of the most effective ways of organizing problem-solving sessions in your classroom is to randomly assign students into groups-of-four. Groups of this size insure that everyone has the opportunity to provide input, and they also enhance the probability that enough "good" ideas will be generated to keep the solution process alive.

Present your class with the problem of breaking into teams so that everyone has an equal chance of being in any one of the groups (random assignment). Such an arrangement may be inconceivable to some children who "can't think without their friends" or "get sick when they sit next to a girl." Dealing with such real-world issues is the stuff "real" understanding is made of. Teachers, who confront these situations daily, should view such activities as ideal opportunities for children to practice their problem-solving skills in a context most meaningful to daily classroom life. Children we worked with have offered several suggestions for breaking into groups (counting off and drawing numbers from a hat; selecting cards from a well shuffled deck of appropriate size); however, your students should be encouraged to develop their own procedures.

Once established, each team can be given a unique problem to work on or a set of problems from which to select. All four team members must work on the same problem. The following rule is the only one we have found necessary to enforce (beyond common sense):

In order to seek help from anyone outside the group-of-four (i.e., the teacher) all four students must agree on the question to be asked.

Initial problem-solving sessions should be relatively brief (15 minutes), followed immediately by a large group discussion of about equal duration. One member from each group should report their progress and ask for suggestions. With experience, longer sessions may be warranted and follow-up sessions may be less frequent, though more intense. It is important that the groups rotate the reporting responsibilities so that everyone has the opportunity to report results to the class.

Groups-of-four offers a flexible problem-solving arrangement for students of all ages. Leadership roles and individual responsibilities are negotiated by the children themselves. Once the groups are functioning, the teacher can sit in on discussions, providing hints and asking critical questions. The groups must work towards consensus, asking for help or reporting results as a unit. Changing group organization frequently (every one to two weeks) encourages flexibility and divergent thinking. Groups-of-four can become an integral part of your school day. Not only will it serve as a vehicle for mathematical problem solving, but it also may assist in resolving other critical classroom issues confronting you and your students throughout the year.

MIND SET

Several psychological factors significantly affect an individual's ability to confront novel problems successfully. As previously discussed, self-confidence and persistence develop as a result of successful experiences with challenges of appropriate difficulty. In turn, they foster an optimistic attitude that problems are essentially solvable. Without such optimism, even the most dedicated individuals will be defeated before they begin.

An additional factor which seems important in developing successful problem-solving skills is mind set. Mind set refers to the level of flexibility an individual exhibits throughout the process of selecting an appropriate course of action. Early in the solution enterprise it is important to maintain an open mind when evaluating competing strategies. Many times we fall into the trap of following a particular solution path just because the scenery is familiar. The better you become at suspending initial judgments and actively seeking novel alternatives, the greater the likelihood of uncovering solutions to unfamiliar problems. Once a likely strategy has been determined, this open mind set gives way to a persistent search for patterns and clues. If the results are disappointing after a reasonable effort, persistence must in turn give way to flexibility in order to once again give competing strategies an opportunity to surface. It is important to maintain an open mind set throughout the first two stages—understanding the problem and designing a solution strategy—described in the next section. The following example suggests the importance of initially viewing problems in an open, holistic manner.

> A steel fitter was told to build a shelf inside the hull of a submarine from the following plans. The diameter of the hull is known to be 10 meters. The draftsman forgot to label the length of the diagonal brace. The worker quickly figured the proper length of the brace without looking at the original blueprint. How?

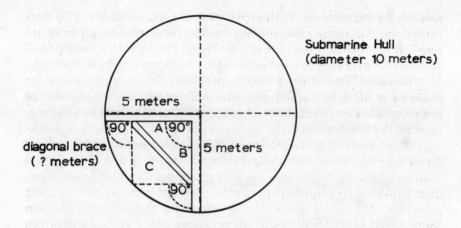

The reader who remembers a bit of high school geometry might begin by applying the Pythagorean theorem ($A^2 + B^2 = C^2$), but will soon see that this approach is fruitless. Establishing a mind set too early in the solution process may cause the solver to focus on unproductive elements within the problem situation. In this case, it is useful to observe that the brace forms the diagonal of a rectangle. Knowing that the diagonals of a rectangle are equal and observing the opposite diagonal is in fact a radius of the hull, it is a simple matter to conclude that the brace is 5 meters long.

A FOUR-STEP PLAN

Polya's general problem solving plan can be described as four separate yet interrelated steps:

1. Understanding the problem
2. Designing a solution strategy
3. Carrying out the strategy
4. Evaluating the results

Step 1: Understanding the Problem

The first step in solving any problem is to understand what is given and what the intended goal is. This is a crucial stage in the solution process. Without a thorough understanding of what is known and where you are headed, the process of determining a solution strategy will be confounded. Understanding the problem situation involves more than reading a few sentences or listening to a story. Not only are the immediate facts important, but related facts and associated known problems as well.

Conditions relevant to the solution must also be described so they can be taken into account. The more practical (i.e., realistic) the problem, the more important are the conditions. For example, if we consider the problems associated with the excessive use of imported oil in the

United States today, one simplistic solution is to legislate radically lower import quotas. This "solution" solves the stated problem, but it violates an equally important implicit condition, namely that we need to reduce imports without destroying our economy in the process. Though these implicit conditions may simply represent a minor complication in some cases, they may relate to a more general problem in others. Regardless, they must be taken into account if any solution is to be considered valid.

Some useful techniques for helping children understand the facts and conditions associated with a problem include:

1. Restating the problem in their own words
2. Listing given information
3. Listing given conditions
4. Writing down the stated goal in their own words
5. Listing related relevant facts
6. Listing implicit conditions
7. Describing related known problems

Step 2: Designing a Solution Strategy

Once the problem situation has been satisfactorily untangled, a solution strategy should be chosen. This step in the plan is often applied prematurely and is a frequent cause of failure. Many times insufficient effort is spent in the initial stage of understanding the problem itself.

Strategies are chosen based on past experience with related problems, insight gathered from the structure of the given information, conditions or goal and perhaps some unexplained inspiration. The teacher can play a vital role at this stage by offering appropriate hints to assist the discovery process. One of the greatest challenges to teachers is to know when to provide guidance and when to allow the struggle to continue unassisted.

One way of viewing this subtle process is to consider that anyone can solve any problem if given sufficient expert assistance. The role of the sensitive teacher, then, is to broaden the student's range of independent problem-solving abilities (zone of proximal development) until the student requires little or no external assistance. This zone of understanding can usually be applied to only a narrow class of problems, though with sufficient experience it may be possible to acquire the ability to transfer skill from one domain to another. An accomplished engineer might more easily learn to be an architect than someone without a similar problem-solving background.

The teacher's task becomes one of recognizing the "teaching moment" and providing a level of guidance appropriate to the ability and experience of the learner. This ability to recognize appropriate points to interject a word of encouragement or an unobtrusive suggestion seems as rare as it is important. Questions should initially be quite general, gradually becoming more specific until the student receives just enough assistance to effectively proceed. Polya suggested that questions and hints should be offered discreetly and be selected in such a manner that they "could have occurred to the student himself." Avoid magic tricks and surprise results. Polya offered several questions which might be used as models for teachers wishing to give children an appropriate share of the work in designing a solution strategy.

Helpful Hints and Questions for Problem Solving

1. What is the goal? What are you trying to find?
2. What information is given? What do you know?
3. What special conditions (restrictions) apply?
4. Try to remember a problem with a similar unknown (goal).
5. Could you use its solution to help in any way?
6. Can you restate the problem in your own words?
7. If you can't solve the problem as stated, can you first solve a similar one?
8. Did you use all the given information?
9. Are there other facts that could be useful?
10. How do the given conditions restrict the solution?

Only as a last resort should the teacher offer specific suggestions like "Maybe you should average these six amounts," or "I think I would try multiplying the number of cars by 4." Remember, learning to solve problems is like traveling—planning is half the fun.

Strategies for Problem Solving

In designing an assault on a novel problem, one or more strategies from the following arsenal should prove to be effective. Most problems succumb to more than one technique, though whole classes of problems may be successfully untangled with the judicious application of one favorite strategy.

Guesstimation.   Trial and error methods are widely used by people of all ages and can be quite efficient for certain types of problems. The technique of using repetitious cycles of successive approximation has received a lot of bad press over the past century or two, generally perpetrated by over-zealous mathematicians seeking "beauty and rigor" in their chosen field. Much of what we know today, however, was motivated by such enthusiastic "messing about." Guesstimation can be thought of as a preliminary, informal experiment motivated by intuition.

Its most obvious advantage, simplicity, makes it well-suited for use by young children. What it gains in common sense application, however, it loses in efficiency. Generally, trial and error methods consume considerable time and effort, yet may provide the only initial entry into a novel situation. It is interesting to note that modern computers utilize adaptations of such techniques in order to compute square roots, trigonometric functions and a host of other fancy tricks. For example:

Suppose you have enough money to build 100 meters of fence to protect your new garden. If you want the largest possible garden, what would be the dimensions of the fence enclosure?

First we list the given facts, conditions and goal:

Fact   —There are 100 meters of fence.

Conditions—The garden must have the largest possible area.
            —There can be no breaks in the fence.
            —The edges of enclosure must add up to 100 meters.

Goal   —Find the dimensions of the enclosure.

Let's try a few initial guesses to help us understand the problem and perhaps discover a pattern. A piece of graph paper will help keep things organized.

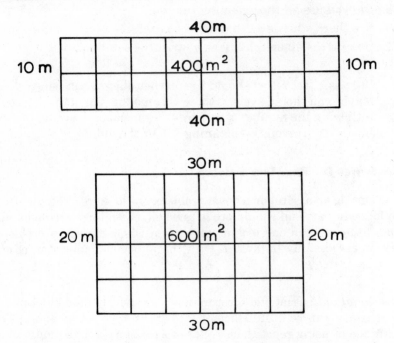

It seems that as the enclosure gets "fatter," more area is available for the garden. Let's try the fattest four-sided figure.

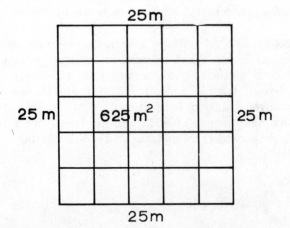

If we are satisfied with a four-sided figure (an implicit condition), a square enclosure seems to afford the most generous garden. If more area is required, enclosures with more or less than four sides might be explored. It is interesting to note that a circle affords the largest garden for any fixed boundary (if you can plow in circles). How much extra planting room does a circular enclosure provide over the square garden?

Working Backwards.   This is one method often used when the solution involves describing the steps which must be taken in order to achieve a stated goal. When using this strategy, one starts with the end result and determines a sequence of necessary preceding conditions (analysis) which, when carried out in reverse (synthesis), will generate the desired result. To be useful, the analysis must proceed towards a known state—something already well understood. This process is useful for various geometric and practical problems. It may provide an initial wedge into an otherwise opaque problem situation. For example:

> A pub normally sells beer in 4- and 9-pint pitchers (the owner refused to convert to metric). An old-time patron was too thirsty for the small pitcher but not thirsty enough for a large one. He asked the bartender to draw him exactly 6 pints. The bartender thought for a few minutes and said, "I can fill your order using only *one 4 pint* and *one 9-pint* pitcher, but I'll have to wait until a couple more customers arrive." How did he do it?

To solve this problem, we again list the given facts, conditions and goal:

   Fact   —We have a 4-pint and a 9-pint pitcher.

Conditions—We have a large quantity of beer available.

            —We don't want to throw away any beer.

   Goal   —Put 6 pints of beer in the 9-pint pitcher.

Working backwards is a convenient strategy for this problem. First we temporarily assume the problem is solved and imagine we have the 6 pints of beer. We can then work backwards looking for necessary preconditions until we arrive at a known condition. We might even try using water in order to conduct an actual experiment.

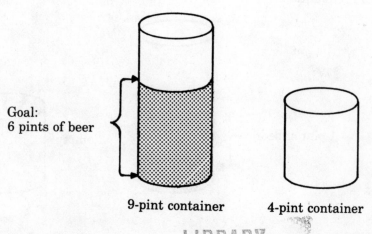

Goal:
6 pints of beer

9-pint container   4-pint container

A sufficient precondition for the goal is to have 1 pint in the small container and the large container full. Then, we could pour off 3 pints by filling the rest of the 4-pint container, leaving 6 pints in the 9-pint container.

1st Precondition:

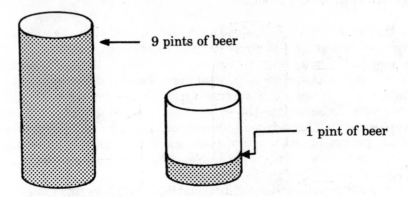

This situation can be easily reached from the situation below.

2nd Precondition:

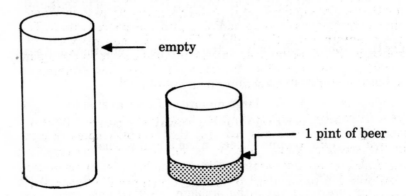

Still working backwards we can easily arrive at the third precondition below.

3rd Precondition:

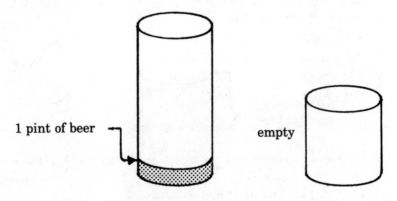

Finally, the third precondition can be reached from the situation below if we realize that we can pour off two 4-pint containers leaving 1 pint in the large container. To avoid wasting any beer a couple of thirsty customers will have to drink these two pitchers before reversing the steps to reach the goal.

4th Precondition: (known state)

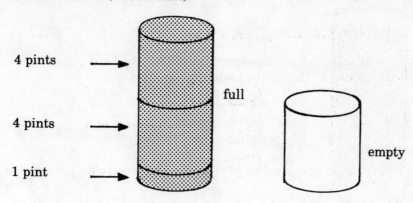

4 pints →

4 pints →   full

1 pint →   empty

SOLUTION. After two customers arrived, the bartender filled the large pitcher, poured off one 4-pint pitcher and served it to a waiting patron. After she finished, the bartender poured off another 4 pints and served it to the other thirsty patron. When the pitcher returned, the remaining pint was poured into it. The large container was then refilled. The small container was subsequently filled by pouring off 3 pints of beer from the 9-pint container, leaving 6 pints. It makes you thirsty just thinking about the plight of the poor bartender.

Reduce to a Simpler Case.   Insight can be gained into many problems by assigning simpler values or reducing the level of complexity specified in the problem. Many times by simply removing the cognitive stress induced by the appearance of large numbers, fractions or decimals, children are better able to concentrate on the fundamental interrelationships between problem elements. Once this simple version is solved, the original values can be substituted and the solution steps repeated. For example:

Suppose you're throwing a party and are planning to serve canned shrimp. Three different size cans are available. Which gives you the best buy?

net weight
1. 227 grams   @ $3.45 a can
2. 341 grams   @ $4.78 a can
3. 454 grams   @ $6.81 a can

What are the given facts, conditions and goal?

　　　Fact 　—Three different size cans are available with different prices.
Conditions—You must buy whole cans.
　　Goal 　—Determine which can offers the best buy.

To develop a rule for finding the best buy, let's use a "model" can with "nice" numbers.

200 grams net weight @ $4.00 a can

It is somewhat easier to determine the price per gram since the answer comes out even.

400 ÷ 200 = 2¢ per gram

Using a calculator, we can follow the same rule with the actual values and discover which can is the best buy.

1. 345 ÷ 227 = 1.5¢ per gram
2. 478 ÷ 341 = 1.4¢ per gram
3. 681 ÷ 454 = 1.5¢ per gram

An additional example where simplifying helps with the solution is described below.

A bank robber was planning his getaway route from the bank to his hideout. He wanted to figure out how many routes were possible and if one was shorter than the rest. He drew the following map to help solve the problem.

Bank

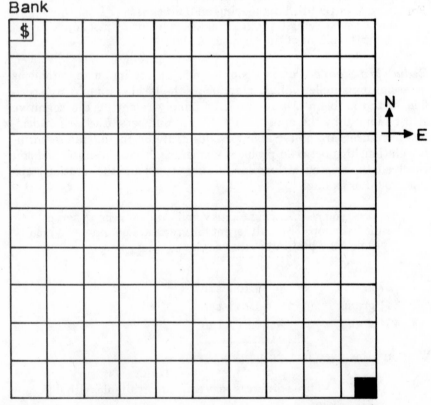

Hideout

The robber has to drive on the streets of the hundred block
section of town and wants to get to the hideout as quickly as
possible (he always has to drive East or South). How many
routes are there and which one is shortest?

To solve this problem, let's first list the given facts, conditions and
goals.

Facts   —We are given a 10 × 10 block section of the city.
         —The blocks are square.

Conditions—The robber must drive on streets.
         —He must drive East or South.

Goals   —Find the total number of routes.
         —Find the shortest route.

Since the number of routes for a 10 × 10 section is quite large, it might
be convenient to look at smaller sections and see if we can discover a
pattern. In a 1 × 1 block section we find two possible routes.

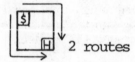

For a 1 × 2 section we find three possible routes.

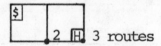

For a 2 × 2 section we find six possible routes. Can you find them?

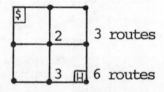

For a 2 × 3 section we find ten routes.

And for a 3 × 3 section we find twenty routes.

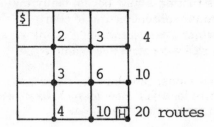

Observing the patterns in the figures above (along with a bit of faith) we can easily complete the problem for a 10 × 10 section. Notice that in order to find the number of possible routes at any corner one needs only to add the number of routes to the corners immediately to the North and to the West of the point in question. (Note that there is only one route to any corner around the outer edge.)

$									
2	3	4	5	6	7	8	9	10	11
3	6	10	15	21	28	36	45	55	66
4	10	20	35	56	84	120	165	220	286
5	15	35	70	126	210	330	495	715	1001
6	21	56	126	252	462	792	1287	2002	3003
7	28	84	210	462	924	1716	3003	5005	8008
8	36	120	330	792	1716	3432	6435	11440	19448
9	45	165	495	1287	3003	6435	12870	24310	43758
10	55	220	715	2002	5005	11440	24310	28620	92378
11	66	286	1001	3002	8008	19448	43758	92378	H

184,756 routes

The robber has 184,756 possible routes to choose from. Without simplifying the problem and looking for patterns, the solution would be time-consuming indeed. How long would it take to "check out" all the routes if only twenty could be driven in one day? It is interesting to note that all the routes are the same length. Can you prove it?

Another frequently used simplification strategy involves breaking a complex problem into smaller, more palatable chunks. Each of the subproblems can then be solved and, when taken together, comprise a solution to the original problem. Just as a builder must concentrate first on the grading, then the foundation, framing, roofing and other elements of constructing a new house, many mathematical problems succumb to a similar subcontracting of effort.

Problems which are susceptible to chunking abound in the fields of measurement and geometry. For example:

> A carpet layer must calculate floor area prior to determining the total price for a job. How many square meters of carpet will be required for the floor plan below?

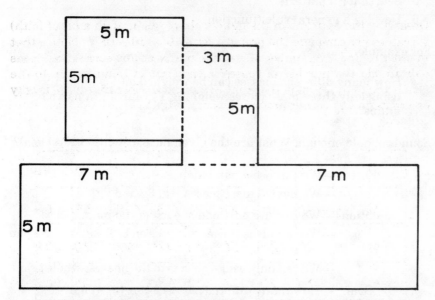

It is useful to break the floor plan into rectangles. Add the results to determine the total floor space.

$$5m \times 5m = 25m^2$$
$$3m \times 5m = 15m^2$$
$$5m \times 17m = \underline{85m^2}$$

Total floor area $125m^2$

Conduct an Experiment. Though most real world problem solving (business, science, engineering) relies heavily on experimentation, elementary aged children are rarely encouraged to conduct experiments as a practical problem solving strategy. Classical experiments (scientific method) are remarkably similar to the four-step general problem solving plan. First, one must understand the problem and define a goal (hypothesis). Next, a strategy must be formulated (design an experiment) and carried out (data collection). Finally, the solver evaluates the results of the experiment(s) and tests the hypothesis for accuracy.

In mathematical problem solving experiments generally consist of carrying out some systematic procedure using a physical material or some sort of graphic representation. Sketches, graphs and tables are useful when organizing data gathered from an experiment. Once the data have been organized, searching for patterns or general rules (functions) usually aids the solution process.

The following list of suggestions is helpful when trying to solve a problem by experimentation. Generally, a coordinated effort using two or more aids is necessary to achieve success.

Aids to use when conducting an experiment:

1. Design a physical model
2. Make a sketch or diagram
3. Collect data and organize it in a table
4. Construct a graph
5. Search for a pattern
6. Develop a general rule (function)

For example:

> How many different masses can be weighed on a pan balance using only three mass pieces weighing 1 gram, 3 grams and 9 grams?

Sounds simple enough. What are the given facts, conditions and goal?

> Facts   —We can use a pan balance.
>
> —We have 3 mass pieces (1g, 3g and 9g).
>
> Conditions—We can use only one of each of the mass pieces.
>
> —We can place the mass pieces on both sides of the pan balance.
>
> —We can only weigh objects to the nearest whole gram.
>
> Goal   —How many different masses can we weigh?

Conducting an experiment will help with the solution. First, let's try weighing some objects with a pan balance.

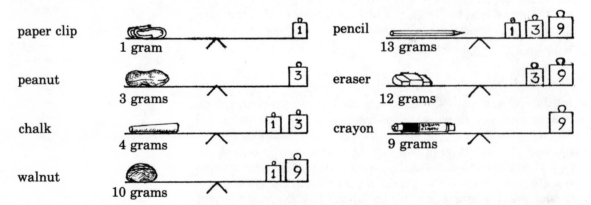

The answer seems to be seven (not including 0 grams), yet if we realize that the conditions allow us to put mass pieces on either or both pans, additional masses can be weighed.

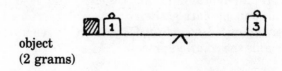

object
(2 grams)

Let's fill in a table in order to list all possible conditions.

Mass weighed (g)	Mass piece on left pan	Mass piece on right pan
1		1 g
2	1 g	3 g
3		3 g
4		1 g & 3 g
5	1 g & 3 g	9 g
6	3 g	9 g
7	3 g	1 g & 9 g
8	1 g	9 g
9		9 g
10		1 g & 9 g
11	1 g	3 g & 9 g
12		3 g & 9 g
13		1 g & 3 g & 9 g

All whole number masses from 1 to 13 grams can be weighed! Try including one 27-gram mass piece along with the original three pieces and determine the number of different masses that can be weighed. What is the minimum number of mass pieces necessary to weigh every whole number mass from 1 to 1000 grams? Can you think of a situation where such a set of mass pieces would be extremely convenient?

Add Elements to the Problem Situation. One final strategy which is rarely used but worthwhile mentioning is the addition of new elements to the problem. A few problems are virtually insolvable without applying this technique. A classic example is the following:

> Suppose you are given a bag full of marbles and are told that all the marbles are identical. You are allowed to take out only one marble at a time to look at, but it must be returned to the bag. Under the stated conditions, how can we accurately estimate the number of marbles in the bag?

If we remain limited to the given elements (bag, marbles, see one marble at a time and return), no solution short of guessing is available. If, however, we break out of our traditional mind set and consider adding a new element to the situation, a solution becomes possible.

> SOLUTION. First remove one marble and carefully observe its characteristics. Find a supply of identical marbles (say, 20) and mark each with an *s*. Return the original marble and the 20 new "seed" marbles to the bag and shake the bag until the "seeds" are thoroughly mixed with the original marbles. Next, conduct an experiment by removing one marble, noting if it is a "seed" or original marble, return it to the bag and shake it thoroughly. Organize the data in a table as below.

Seed Marbles	Original Marbles

After sufficient trials, the laws of probability inform us that for every 20 seed marbles (the total number seeded) we draw, we will have also drawn out the number of original marbles in the bag! For example if in 100 trials we drew out 40 seed marbles and 60 original marbles, we predict that there were 30 marbles originally in the bag. Remember, for each set of 20 seed marbles drawn ($2 \times 20 = 40$) we should have drawn out the number of original marbles in the bag ($2 \times 30 = 60$).

The word "sufficient" is very important here since a sample of 10 or 20 marbles is not large enough to allow the laws of probability to be predictive. Samples of 100 to 500 should do the trick if the bag is shaken well. It is interesting to note that there is no guarantee of drawing *every* seed or original marble no matter how large the sample. The proportion of seed to original marbles is what we're really looking for. It is even possible (though very remote) that the same seed and original marble are repeatedly drawn throughout the experiment!

This process of seeding is used in medical diagnosis of various blood diseases. A radioactive material which is absorbed by healthy and diseased cells in differing proportions is injected into the blood stream. By measuring the ratio between the radioactivity of healthy and diseased cells, an accurate count of diseased cells can be established.

The solution to our problem in submarine geometry further illustrates the usefulness of this technique. By inserting the opposite diagonal into the diagram, the solution becomes trivial; since both braces are equal and the new one is a radius of the circle (5 meters), the original brace must also be 5 meters long.

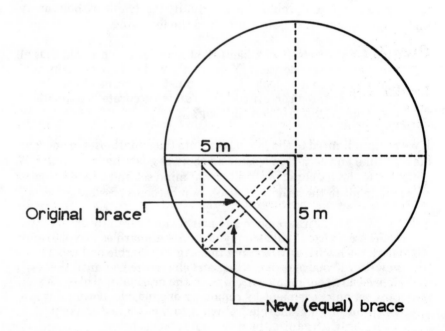

Step 3: Carrying Out the Strategy

Once the problem situation is understood (facts, conditions and goal) and the difficult task of devising a solution strategy has been completed, the next step is to get your feet wet and apply the chosen strategy. It should be pointed out that in practice, Steps 1, 2 and 3 are not carried out in isolation from each other but in fact may be far more interdependent than is apparent. In trying to understand a problem, it may be useful to immediately apply a favorite strategy and gather a bit of data which may, in turn, further understanding of the problem and lead to an effective solution strategy. Initially, however, novices should proceed through the steps as described and yet try not to get stuck at any one step.

Carrying out a solution strategy primarily requires persistence. The task is to determine whether or not the chosen strategy generates meaningful clues towards unraveling the problem. These clues may take the form of patterns or general rules relating the problem to a known example.

Throughout the process of working through a strategy it is important to:

1. Keep accurate records (tables, sketches, etc.)
2. Stick to the chosen strategy until some evidence suggests specific changes
3. Carefully monitor each step in the solution for accuracy
4. If no headway is made after a reasonable period of time, put the problem aside for a day or two, then try it again or look for another strategy.

Step 4: Evaluating the Results

Looking back over the solution of a problem is beneficial for two reasons. First, it provides an opportunity to evaluate and refine the results. Second, it brings the process of solution into clear focus. At no time are children in a better position to clearly understand and explain the somewhat intuitive processes in which they are engaged than immediately following a successful problem-solving experience. Not only does the child evaluate the validity of the results, but more importantly, coordinates the current solution with previously solved problems.

Nothing causes problems like solutions; the real benefit to the learner extends much farther than the immediate result of any particular problem. If each solution is carefully reconsidered in light of past experience and coordinated with prior results, the ability to solve novel problems in the future may be enhanced. If the goal is to improve general problem-solving abilities, children must be strongly encouraged to reexamine their successes, refine their results, and *imagine problems which have been or could be solved* with similar techniques. Otherwise each problem is but a lonely star shining in the unknown.

SUMMARY: GENERAL PROBLEM-SOLVING PLAN

Step I. Understand the problem.
        A. Know the given facts, conditions and goal.

Step II. Design a solution strategy.
        A. Use guesstimation (trial and error).
        B. Work backwards.
        C. Reduce to simpler case.
        D. Conduct an experiment.
            1. Design a physical model.
            2. Make a sketch or diagram.
            3. Collect data and organize it in a table.
            4. Construct a graph.
            5. Search for a pattern.
            6. Develop a general rule (function).
        E. Add elements to the problem situation.

Step III. Carry out the strategy.
        A. Persistently follow through with the solution strategy.
        B. Maintain accurate record of the data collected, etc.

Step IV. Evaluate the results.
        A. If a solution is uncovered, refine the results and try to relate them to other problems.
        B. If not, reevaluate your understanding and seek a new solution strategy.

SECTION **II**

Classroom Problem-Solving Kit

WHOLE CLASS PROBLEM-SOLVING WARM-UPS

BREAKING INTO GROUPS-OF-FOUR

Present the problem of dividing the class into groups-of-four with each student having an equal chance of being in any group. In a teacher-directed large-group discussion, have the class brainstorm possible random selection techniques and then discuss the effects of each suggestion. Start by listing all the suggestions on the board without comment. Then, each suggestion should be carefully discussed and the most effective methods chosen.

Some possible suggestions for a class of thirty-two include:

1. Deal out an appropriate sized, shuffled deck of cards and form groups of people with the same number.
2. Alphabetize the class list and count off by fours.
3. Draw names out of a hat, four at a time.
4. Have students draw out of a hat containing four sets of cards numbered one through eight. Those with the same number go together.

BRAINSTORMING

Have the whole class work together to "brainstorm" possible answers, using questions similar to those below. Write responses on a piece of poster board or on the blackboard. Discuss each response in detail, making sure everyone has an opportunity for input.

1. Name 10 things that come in millions.
2. Name 10 things that you can do with a blade of grass.
3. If you had to leave home quickly and could only take one suitcase with you, what would you put in it?
4. This school would be a better place if everyone . . .
5. Name 10 things you can do with a pencil sharpener.
6. List 10 words that describe this class.
7. List 10 things you can do now that you couldn't do last year.
8. Make up an interesting question for the class to brainstorm.

MIND READING

Ask each student in your class to think of a number between 0 and 50. Both digits must be odd and they cannot be alike. For example, you cannot use 11. Have each student secretly write his or her number on a piece of paper.

Before starting the activity, secretly write the number 37 on the board and cover it with a piece of paper. After the whole class has written down its guesses, ham it up a bit, asking them to concentrate on their numbers so you can read their minds. Dramatically remove the paper covering the number on the board and ask how many students chose the number 37. A surprising number of students will probably have chosen this number.

Try the same activity again, but ask for a number between 50 and 100 made up of two different *even* digits. This time write the digits 6 and 8 on two large cards (or use playing cards). Again ask them to concentrate, and then show them the number 68. Many will have chosen this number. Reverse the cards and explain that they may have gotten their wires crossed if they chose 86.

Though this seems like a magic act, in fact there are only eight numbers that fit the first category and for some curious psychological reason, most people choose 37 (the next most popular number is 35). The second situation is restricted to eight choices as well, with 68 being the most popular. Of course, reversing the cards to show 86 thereby increases your mind-reading success.

RACE TO 21

Race to 21 is played by two people taking turns counting one or two numbers until someone reaches 21. Choose who is to start. The first person can either say "1" or "1, 2." The other contestant counts on from where the first person left off (again saying one or two numbers). This process of alternate counting continues until 21 is reached. The winner is the person who says 21. This game can be played with all ages and various sized groups. The teacher should play against volunteers in the class to help students learn the counting procedure. Then have the children pair off and see if they can develop a winning strategy.

A clever way to unravel this problem is to play the game backwards. If you want to say 21, which previous number must you say? If you say 18, your opponent could count "19," or "19, 20." Either way, you could claim 21. If you must say 18, which previous number must you say? This time 15 is the key number since saying it guarantees you can claim 18. Continue this process. If you say 3 you are guaranteed all the key numbers to 21. To say 3 your opponent must start (unless you are very lucky). However, if you have been chosen to start, try to capture a key number as soon as possible. Once you say a multiple of 3, you are guaranteed to be a winner (if you don't make any mistakes).

Once your students have mastered this version, try counting one, two or *three* numbers at a time. Another interesting twist is to make 21 "poison"—the person who says 21 loses.

PICO-FERMI-NADA

The goal of Pico-Fermi-Nada is to guess a secret three digit number. The leader writes any three digit number on a piece of paper and hides it. Individuals or teams take turns guessing three digit numbers. Each time someone guesses, the leader gives one of the clues below:

1. Pico—At least one digit is correct and in the correct position.
2. Fermi—At least one digit is correct but is in the wrong position.
3. Nada—No digits are correct.

Try to guess the secret number in the fewest possible attempts. Teams can play against each other, alternating guesses and learning the clues from each other. The whole class can also play as a unit trying to reduce the number of guesses from one trial to the next.

Here is a sample game: Secret number (714).

	Guess	Clue—Comments
1	987	Fermi—At least one digit correct but in wrong position.
2	999	Nada—No digit correct (9 is not a digit in the secret number).
3	888	Nada—No digit correct (8 is not a digit in the secret number).
4	978	Fermi—7 is a correct digit but must be in the first position.
5	654	Pico—At least one digit is correct (6 is not a digit in the secret number).
6	235	Nada—2, 3, and 5 are not digits in the secret number.
7	714	Pico, Pico, Pico—(Guesser could have guessed 704 or 764, requiring additional clues.)

The comments in the preceding table provide examples of logical deductions which can be made after each guess and clue. With experience, guesses can be carefully chosen to provide as much information as possible from each of the clues. With practice, any three digit number can be "guessed" in 7 to 10 tries.

CAR RACE

Show your class how to graph coordinate pairs before playing Car Race. Beginning at (0,0) on the following coordinate graph, explain that the first number in the pair (3,4) tells you to go right three spaces and the second tells you to go up four spaces. The car shows you where to end up.

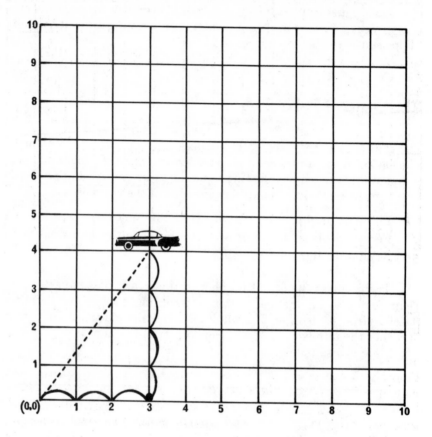

To play Car Race, draw a wide road on a piece of 1 cm squared paper. Each player begins at the starting line. They each have their own (0,0) starting coordinate. To race, each player in turn can add (or subtract) 1 from his/her first *or* second coordinate and move his/her car to the spot indicated by the new coordinate pair. Notice each person starts at (0,0), so the only two first moves are (0,1) or (1,0) for all the players. (Avoid negative numbers until the class decides they need them later in the problem. See the following example.) After everyone has moved once, again add (or subtract) 1 to either coordinate and move on from the last position. Continue adding (or subtracting) 1 to each subsequent move and try to negotiate the curves without crashing into the edge of the road or another car. The first one to the finish line without crashing is the winner.

Sample Car Race Game

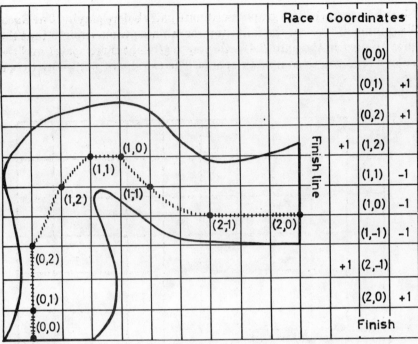

Begin by having the whole class race one car. Later, break into groups of two or three and have the students work on efficient strategies by racing against each other.

Remember to consider the current position of each car as (0,0) and move on as indicated by the new coordinate pair. Notice that each time 1 is added to one of the coordinates the car moves "faster" and may change direction slightly. Subtracting 1 has the opposite effect. Continue adding (or subtracting) 1 on each subsequent move. Each time remember to consider your current position as (0,0), then move as directed by the new coordinate pair. Try to negotiate the curves without crashing into the edge of the road or another car. Be careful not to accelerate too rapidly or you won't be able to turn in time to avoid a crash. Play a few practice games and see if you can get to the finish line without a mishap. Whoever gets there first wins.

PROBLEMS
AND
SOLUTIONS

TOOTH TRUTHS

(Problem Starter Sheet 1, page 103)

Which class in your school is missing the most teeth? Fill in the table to help you find out.

Teacher	Grade	Missing Teeth

SOLUTION: TOOTH TRUTHS

Understand the Problem

Facts —Little kids lose a lot of teeth in primary school.

Conditions—Assume that the number of missing teeth averages out about the same over the whole year for any class.

Goal —Find out which class is missing the most teeth.

Design a Solution Strategy

Have groups of students interview children in other classrooms and collect data on the number of missing teeth. Keep track of the grade levels as well. Compile all the data on a chart or the blackboard.

Carry Out Plan

Arrange with the other teachers to expect "visitors" at a specified time. Students in small groups should record the tooth facts on their tables and return to their class for a large group discussion. (Don't forget to count missing teeth in your own class.) Graph the results on a classroom chart by grade level to make comparisons easier.

Evaluate Results

The results will vary somewhat according to the time of year, but when the number of missing teeth is totaled by grade level, the first grade should come out ahead. The graph should help your class make comparisons across classes. You should discuss the need to sample groups of equal size if the comparisons are to be meaningful. Clearly, if you interview twice as many second graders as first the resulting graph will be misleading.

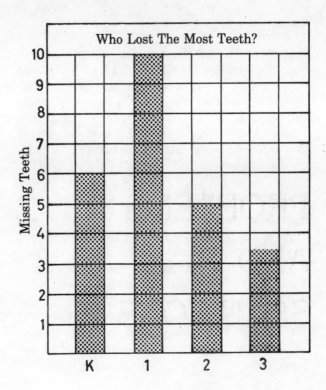

Problem and Solution 2

FRUIT FACTS
(Problem Starter Sheet 2, page 104)

Oranges are a famous fruit first found in China. They come in many sizes and colors. Some have thick skins, some thin. Some are sweet while others are bitter. Do all oranges have the same number of sections? How many seeds are in an orange? Does it matter if they are big or small? See if you can find out.

Conditions—All oranges may not have the same number of seeds or sections. Try different types and sizes.

Goal —Find out how many seeds and sections are in an orange.

SOLUTION: FRUIT FACTS

Understand the Problem

Facts —There are many types of oranges.

Design a Solution Strategy

Much can be learned about the characteristics and uses of oranges by talking with the local grocer. It is important as well for children to begin utilizing the learning resources available throughout the community. If children have oranges in their lunches, have them conduct an experiment by carefully peeling their oranges and counting the seeds and sections.

Carry Out Plan

This part will vary from region to region. However, encourage your children to actually visit the supermarket and talk with produce people. The results of the experiment should show that small and large oranges of the same type have the same number of sections, though the seed count will vary somewhat. Our last orange had thirteen sections and six seeds.

Evaluate Results

Perhaps the most important result is for your students to begin seeing other people in the community as learning resources. The grocer, the mechanic, and the hairdresser all have a story to tell if you just know the right questions to ask.

It is interesting to note as well that this problem has no one "right" answer. Many right answers can be expressed depending on the type of orange. Other factors such as what constitutes a whole section or how big does a seed have to be to count is the stuff engineering problem solvers work with daily. Try making a classroom graph by gluing the seeds on a piece of poster board as below:

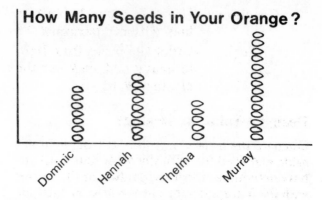

How Many Seeds in Your Orange?

With a bit of imagination, a whole series of fruity problems can be manufactured to give meaning to those rainy-day classroom lunches.

Problem and Solution 3

MYSTERY MASSES
(Problem Starter Sheet 3, page 105)

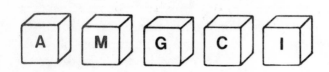

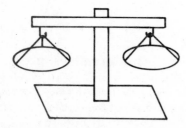

Put the boxes in order from lightest to heaviest.

Below, write the *mystery word* the boxes spell:

 _____ _____ _____ _____ _____

light   heavy

SOLUTION: MYSTERY MASSES

Teacher Note: Using five identical boxes (35 mm slide boxes work well), prepare the mystery masses by putting varying amounts of sand in each. Make sure there is a sufficient difference in mass to tip the scale for any pair of boxes. Order the boxes from light to heavy and letter the boxes M A G I C. Mix them up on the table and set small groups to work with the pan balance.

Understand the Problem

Facts —Five identical boxes are each filled with a different amount of sand.

Conditions—Use only a pan balance to help with comparisons.

Goal —Order the boxes from light to heavy and spell out the mystery word.

Design a Solution Strategy

Compare the mass of any pair. Set the light one aside and continue with the other four until you have determined the heaviest. Repeat the process with the four remaining boxes and so on until you have all the boxes in order.

Carry Out Plan

Here are the results of the first cycle of comparisons:

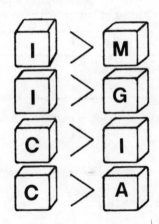

Therefore, *C* is the heaviest. The next cycle might give these results:

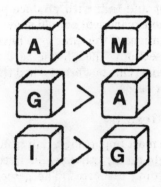

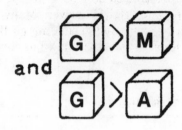

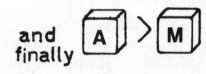

Therefore, *I* is the next heaviest, then *G*, *A*, and *M*.

Evaluate Results

The mystery word is M A G I C. It is possible to order a set of five objects in 4 + 3 + 2 + 1 = 10 comparisons. How many comparisons would it take for six objects? Seven? Have your class bring in identical small containers (one-serving cereal boxes or ½-pint milk cartons) and construct their own set of mystery masses. Have them letter the boxes with a favorite word or name and give to a friend to solve.

APPLE SHARING

(Problem Starter Sheet 4, page 106)

You will need:

you:

two friends:

one apple:

Share the apple so that you and your two friends get the same amount.

How many seeds are in the apple?
Do all apples have the same number of seeds?
Put the seeds in the sun for a few days. Plant them and see what happens.

SOLUTION: APPLE SHARING

Understand the Problem

Facts —There are three people and one apple.

Conditions—You can cut the apple into as many pieces as desired.

Goal —Divide the apple into three equal pieces, so everyone is happy with his or her share. Count the number of seeds and determine if all apples have the same number.

Design a Solution Strategy

Each person takes a turn cutting the apple into three equal quantities. There may be lots of little pieces. The last person to cut the apple also chooses last.

To find out if all apples have the same number of seeds, students should talk with the grocer (have them try interviewing different ones in the community) and check the number of seeds in several types of apples. Dry the seeds and plant them.

Carry Out Plan

The process of dividing into thirds described here should be tried by several groups of three and discussed.

When counting seeds, students should keep a record in a table as below:

Type of Apple	Number of Seeds
1. Red Delicious	9
2.	
3.	
4.	

Evaluate Results

This set of open ended problems gives children an opportunity to see that problems can sometimes be solved better cooperatively. Also in this process, the concept of one third is developed.

The seed problem offers additional practice observing, organizing and predicting, all of which are important in living our everyday lives. Children may also come to appreciate the knowledge other members of the community have to offer and consequently seek them out as learning resources. Our most recent apple, by the way, had nine seeds. Our experience has shown that the number for various types of eating apples does not vary greatly from this sample. We have had mixed results planting apple seeds. Try drying enough seeds so each student can plant three or four. If you're lucky and the seeds are carefully taken care of, some should sprout.

CLAY BOATS
(Problem Starter Sheet 5, page 107)

You will need:

clay:

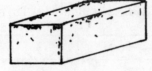

water:

marbles:

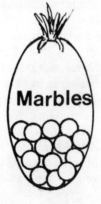

Can you make a clay boat that floats?
Try it.
See how many marbles it will carry.

SOLUTION:
CLAY BOATS

Understand the Problem

Facts —Use a piece of modeling clay.

Conditions—Everyone uses the same amount of clay.

Goal —Make a clay boat that floats and see how many marbles it will carry.

Design a Solution Strategy

Using a trial-and-error strategy, have each student "pinch" out a boat and try to float it in a pail of water. Stop periodically to discuss partial or complete successes. Once everyone has a boat floating, distribute marbles to see which boat can "float" the most marbles.

Carry Out Plan

Discussing success throughout the trial-and-error period should help shape future designs and make the whole process more efficient. Fundamentally, this group problem solving process got us to the moon.

Evaluate Results

Most children, given time and encouragement, will construct a "floater." More efficient boats will have thin walls and maximum interior volumes. Half of a sphere is theoretically the most effective shape and should carry the most marbles.

CHANGING CHANGE
(Problem Starter Sheet 6, page 108)

How many ways can you make change for 16¢?

SOLUTION:
CHANGING CHANGE

Understand the Problem

Facts — Use dimes, nickels and pennies.

Conditions — You do not need to use all three types of coins each time.

Goal — Find all the ways to make change for 16¢.

Design a Solution Strategy

Using make-believe or real money, find a combination of coins equaling 16¢ using the largest coins first. Record the results in the table. Continue making new combinations always using the largest possible until you reach sixteen pennies. Some children may find it easier to draw the coins instead of recording the results numerically.

Carry Out Plan

The table below lists all the ways to make change for 16¢.

	10¢	5¢	1¢	
1.	1 dime	1 nickel	1 penny	= 16¢
2.	1		6	= 16¢
3.		3	1	= 16¢
4.		2	6	= 16¢
5.		1	11	= 16¢
6.			16	= 16¢

Evaluate Results

There are six ways to make 16¢ using dimes, nickels and pennies. This activity gives students practice with systematically searching for all possible combinations. It is a very difficult task for many young children to locate all the combinations and know when they have finished. After individuals or groups have worked on the problem, a whole-class discussion is in order.

More complex money problems can be easily posed by increasing the total amount slightly. There are nine ways to make 21¢ and 782 ways to make $1.21! (See Money Matters, page 73.) Limit the types of coins or total amounts in order to keep the number of combinations reasonable.

CANDY BARS
(Problem Starter Sheet 7, page 109)

Here are some whole candy bars:

Here are some candy bars with bites out of them. These are not whole candy bars:

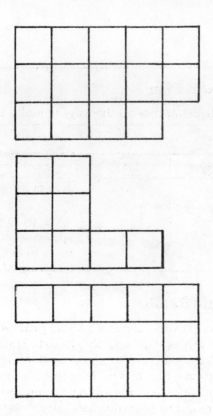

No candy bar can have more than nine units on an edge:

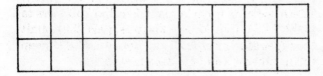

How many different whole candy bars can you make?

SOLUTION: CANDY BARS

Understand the Problem

Facts —Candy bars are rectangular arrays of small squares with no bites out of them.

—A (2,3) candy bar is considered the same as a (3,2) candy bar.

Conditions—No candy bar can be larger than 9 units on any edge.

Goal —Find the total number of different candy bars.

Design a Solution Strategy

Using 1 cm squared paper, cut out all possible candy bars from 1 to 9 units on an edge. Use a systematic procedure to insure that no candy bars are skipped. Keep in mind that just rotating a candy bar does not make it different. For example, the candy bars below are *not* different:

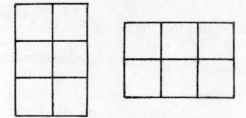

Record the results in a table to ease counting.

Carry Out Plan

The table below shows all possible candy bars with 1 to 9 units on an edge.

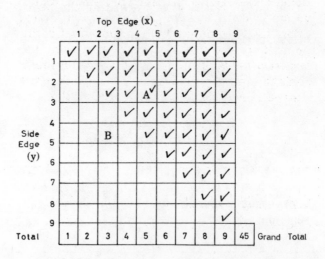

	Top Edge (x)										
	1	2	3	4	5	6	7	8	9		
1	✓	✓	✓	✓	✓	✓	✓	✓	✓		
2		✓	✓	✓	✓	✓	✓	✓	✓		
3			✓	✓	A✓	✓	✓	✓	✓		
4				✓	✓	✓	✓	✓	✓		
5			B		✓	✓	✓	✓	✓		
6						✓	✓	✓	✓		
7							✓	✓	✓		
8								✓	✓		
9									✓		
Total	1	2	3	4	5	6	7	8	9	45	Grand Total

(Side Edge (y) labels the rows.)

Teacher Note: The check marks indicate a candy bar of length (x) and height (y): (3,5) = A. Notice that only the top part of the table is filled in with check marks. The unchecked boxes correspond to the rotated candy bars: (5,3) = B. The number of checks in each column is totaled at the bottom and the grand total is shown on the right.

Evaluate Results

There are exactly 45 different candy bars with edges 1 to 9 units in length. An interesting extension of this problem involves finding a pattern for the number of possible candy bars using different maximum edge lengths. The table below lists the results of several experiments using maximum edge lengths of one through nine.

Maximum Edge Length	Pattern	Number of Candy Bars
1	1	= 1
2	1 + 2	= 3
3	1 + 2 + 3	= 6
4	1 + 2 + 3 + 4	= 10
5	1 + 2 + 3 + 4 + 5	= 15
6	1 + 2 + 3 + 4 + 5 + 6	= 21
7	1 + 2 + 3 + 4 + 5 + 6 + 7	= 28
8	1 + 2 + 3 + 4 + 5 + 6 + 7 + 8	= 36
9	1 + 2 + 3 + 4 + 5 + 6 + 7 + 8 + 9	= 45

A clear pattern is evident. The total number of candy bars with a maximum of 20 units on an edge should be $1 + 2 + 3 + \ldots + 20 = 210$ candy bars. Some of your students may enjoy trying to figure out a shortcut to adding all those numbers together, especially for large candy bars (i.e., 1000 on an edge). Notice that by writing the series $1 + 2 + 3 + 4 + 5 + 6 + 7 + 8 + 9 + 10$ as below and adding pairs, we get a total of five elevens or $5 \times 11 = 55$. Does this pattern always work?

$$
\begin{array}{rccccc}
 & 1 & 2 & 3 & 4 & 5 \\
+ & 10 & 9 & 8 & 7 & 6 \\
\hline
 & 11 & 11 & 11 & 11 & 11 \\
\end{array}
$$

Your students may notice that it is unnecessary to rewrite the sequence of numbers. In the case above, the numbers 5 and 11 can be found by inspection:

$$\tfrac{1}{2} \times 10 = 5$$
$$10 + 1 = 11, \text{ therefore } 5 \times 11 = 55$$

where 10 is the largest number in the series. To find the sum of all the whole numbers from 1 to 20 we follow the same process:

$$\tfrac{1}{2} \times 20 = 10$$
$$20 + 1 = 21, \text{ therefore } 10 \times 21 = 210$$

So $1 + 2 + 3 + \ldots + 20 = 10 \times 21 = 210$. Similarly,

$$1 + 2 + 3 + \ldots + 50 = 25 \times 51 = 1275$$
$$1 + 2 + 3 + \ldots + 15 = 7.5 \times 16 = 120$$

Have your class experiment with several different series to see if the rule always seems to work.

CLASS ALLOWANCE
(Problem Starter Sheet 8, page 110)

How much money does your class spend in a year?

SOLUTION:
CLASS ALLOWANCE

Understand the Problem

Facts —Many children in the United States don't realize how much money they spend.

Conditions—Include only money that children actually spend themselves (not money spent "on" them).

Goal —Find out how much the whole class spends in a year.

Design a Solution Strategy

Individuals or small groups work out their spending habits for a year. Approximate weekly income and spending should be estimated for each student. If necessary, discuss different spending trends during the summer and holidays. Savings should be subtracted. Use a calculator to total spending for whole class and multiply by 52 to find yearly consumer power.

Carry Out Plan

Have each student total up personal spending for one week. Include milk and lunch money, allowance or earnings spent on school supplies, food, toys, comic books, etc. It will be necessary to discuss approximation and estimation skills. Your class will need to understand what "average spending per week" means as well.

Once everyone has computed their estimated average weekly spending, organize the results in a table and have the class fill in their own personal record sheets as well. Have each student compute the class total for a week and multiply by 52 to find their yearly consumer power. Encourage the use of calculators for these computations.

Evaluate Results

This problem clearly demonstrates the usefulness of gathering statistics in order to investigate an everyday occurrence. Your class (and you) may be surprised at the amount of purchasing power in the 5–12-year-old segment of our society. (Saturday morning T.V. advertiseres would not be surprised, however.) The results of this problem can provide the basis for a most interesting values clarification activity to help children make responsible decisions in the marketplace.

PENCIL SURVIVAL

(Problem Starter Sheet 9, page 111)

How long does a pencil last in your class? To find out you will need:

pencils

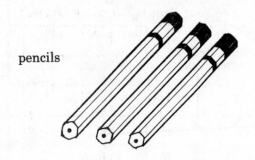

tape

calculator

SOLUTION: PENCIL SURVIVAL

Understand the Problem

Facts —Pencils are used up at an alarming rate in most classrooms.

Conditions—It is assumed the pencils sampled are used up at an average rate.

Goal —Find the average survival rate for a pencil in your class.

Design a Solution Strategy

Label ten new pencils with the date of first use. When the pencil is used up (i.e., too short to sharpen), record the results in a table. After the life span of all ten pencils has been recorded, find the average survival time by dividing the total number of days in use by the number of pencils.

Carry Out Plan

The table below shows the life span of ten pencils. Use a calendar to help count the days and compute the average life span. Remember not to count weekends or holidays when the pencils are resting.

Date First Sharpened	Date Used Up	Number of School Days Used (Subtract)
1. Sept 15	Sept 19	5
2. Sept 15	Sept 18	4
3. Sept 18	Sept 21	5 don't count weekend
4. Sept 18	Sept 22	3 don't count weekend
5. Sept 18	Sept 29	8 don't count weekend
6. Sept 22	Sept 25	4
7. Sept 22	Sept 30	7 don't count weekend
8. Sept 22	Sept 23	2
9. Sept 22	Oct 6	11 don't count weekend
10. Sept 22	Sept 26	5
	Total	54

To find the average life span, divide the total number of days by the number of pencils: $54 \div 10 = 5.4$ days.

Evaluate Results

For this sample, the life span of a pencil was a little over five days. If the sample is representative of normal pencil usage, the average life span may be quite accurate. Sampling more pencils over a longer period of time would offer more reliable results, if desired. Try graphing the pencil life span results as below.

Older children might enjoy computing and graphing a weekly pencil life average to see how their conservation effects change over time.

A discussion of how to "read" and interpret graphs would be appropriate at this time. Include terms like baseline, axis, range and mean (average).

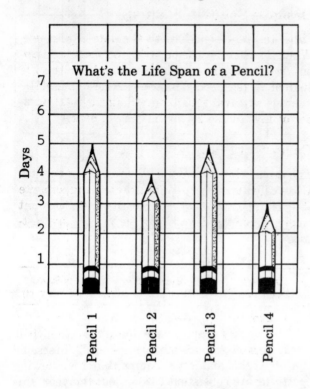

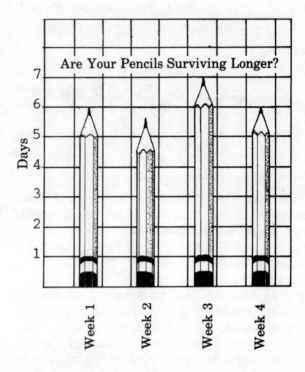

Problem and Solution 10

T.V. HOURS

(Problem Starter Sheet 10, page 112)

How much television do you watch in one year?

SOLUTION: T.V. HOURS

Understand the Problem

Facts —Families watch varying amounts of television.

Conditions—The period sampled should be an average week of T.V. viewing.

—The results will depend on how "average" the week is.

Goal —Determine the number of T.V. viewing hours in one year.

Design a Solution Strategy

Each student should record the number of his or her T.V. viewing hours for one week. Results for one week multiplied by 52 determines the annual T.V. time commitment.

Carry Out Plan

The table below is a record of one week's viewing:

	T.V. Hours
Monday	3
Tuesday	2
Wednesday	3
Thursday	4
Friday	2
Saturday	6
Sunday	5
Total for week	25
Total for year (× 52)	1300

Evaluate Results

This student watched about 1300 hours of television in one year. If more or less television viewing took place during the week sampled than throughout the rest of the year, the total viewing hours would of course be inaccurate. However, for our purposes, the estimate is probably accurate enough. If more accurate results are desired, sample two or three randomly chosen weeks throughout the year and compute the total based on the average of these weekly figures. Some discussion of differing viewing habits during holidays might also be necessary.

It is also fun to compute the number of hours students are engaged in school, eating, playing, and sleeping. The results can easily be graphed as shown below, offering a clear picture of life patterns. Each child can construct a personal graph, or an average class graph can be developed to show overall patterns. For younger children, construct the graph based on one week's activities.

What Is Your Life's Pattern?

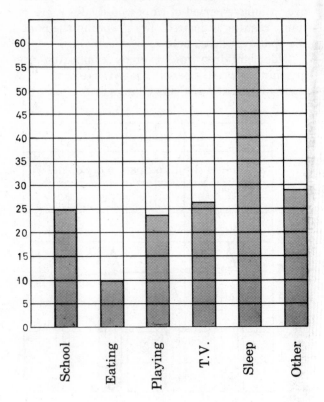

The weekly graph above doesn't tell the whole story, however. Since school is generally in session for 36 weeks, and if we assume that T.V. viewing patterns are consistent throughout the year, this student attended school for only 900 hours and watched 1300 hours of television . . . an excellent topic for discussion.

Other topics of interest which can be effectively investigated using graphs include favorite foods, pets, T.V. programs and sports heroes, number of brothers and sisters, and a favorite of ours—a birthday graph! (Also see Tooth Truths, page 27.)

HOT LUNCH

(Problem Starter Sheet 11, page 113)

Which school lunch does your class like best?

SOLUTION: HOT LUNCH

Understand the Problem

Facts —Some hot lunches are more popular than others.

—Students either bring lunch from home (brownbaggers) or order hot lunch (buyers).

Conditions—It is assumed that a monthly menu is available to the children ahead of time so free choices can be made.

Goal —Find out which foods are the most popular.

Design a Solution Strategy

Keep a record of the types of food served each day, the number of buyers and the number of brownbaggers. Using a calculator, compute the percent of students buying lunch for each food item. To compute the percent, simply divide the number of buyers by the total number of students. If an item is served more than once during the month, find the total number of students buying and divide by the total number of students for all the days the item was served. The calculator will show the answer in decimal form. For our purposes we will round to the first two digits. For example:

$$22 \div 32 = 0.6875 = \frac{69}{100} = 69\%.$$

Carry Out Plan

The table below shows the lunch buying habits of a class for one month.

Menu

	Monday	Tuesday	Wednesday	Thursday	Friday	
Week 1	*Hamburger* Buy 25 Bring 7 Total 32	*Taco* Buy 18 Bring 14 Total 32	*Spaghetti* Buy 21 Bring 11 Total 32	*Pizza* Buy 28 Bring 4 Total 32	*Sloppy Joe* Buy 12 Bring 20 Total 32	
2	*Italian Sandwich* Buy 23 Bring 9 Total 32	*Hot Dog* Buy 15 Bring 16 Total 31	*Pizza* Buy 29 Bring 2 Total 31	*Macaroni* Buy 5 Bring 26 Total 31	*Peanut Butter Sandwich* Buy 25 Bring 7 Total 32	
3	*Sloppy Joe* Buy 10 Bring 22 Total 32	*Hamburger* Buy 21 Bring 9 Total 30	*Spaghetti* Buy 19 Bring 10 Total 30	*Taco* Buy 16 Bring 15 Total 31	*Hot Dog* Buy 18 Bring 12 Total 30	
4	*Pizza* Buy 29 Bring 3 Total 32	*Taco* Buy 20 Bring 12 Total 32	*Italian Sandwich* Buy 20 Bring 10 Total 30	*Hamburger* Buy 23 Bring 9 Total 32	*Macaroni* Buy 8 Bring 23 Total 31	

Organizing the results according to food type, the table below gives a clear picture of food preference.

Type of Food	Total Buyers	Total Students	Percent (Buyers ÷ Total Students)
Hamburger	69	94 (3 days)	73%
Taco	54	95 (3 days)	57%
Spaghetti	40	61 (2 days)	66%
Pizza	86	95 (3 days)	91%
Sloppy Joe	22	64 (2 days)	34%
Italian Sandwich	43	62 (2 days)	69%
Hot Dog	33	61 (2 days)	54%
Macaroni	13	62 (2 days)	21%
Peanut Butter Sandwich	25	32 (1 day)	78%

(Note: Percents are rounded off to the nearest whole percent.)

Graphing the percents in order from small to large helps show the food preferences more clearly.

What Do We Put In Our Bodies?

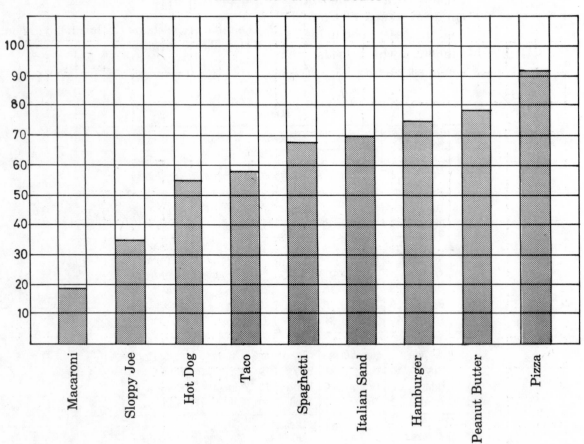

Evaluate Results

Clearly, pizza takes first place in the hot lunch popularity contest. Peanut butter sandwich came in a close second, though we must be careful in interpreting this result, since it was offered only once during the month. Perhaps a late PTA meeting the night before made it difficult for Mom and Dad to pack a lunch at home, so more school lunches would have been bought even if it was liver and onions.

Organizing the percentage graph from least to most gives a clearer picture of the food preferences. Similar graphs can be constructed to help explain other likes and dislikes. For example, try gathering data on sports and recreational preferences, election predictions or opinions on school rules. Evaluations of such attitudinal experiments can provide your students with motivating opportunities to practice analytical skills and strategies for real-world decision making.

Problem and Solution 12

FOLDING BOXES

(Problem Starter Sheet 12, page 114)

Which of these twelve figures will fold into an open-top box? Fold only on dotted lines.

SOLUTION: FOLDING BOXES

Understand the Problem

Facts —There are twelve different figures made up of five squares connected to each other along at least one edge.
—Some figures fold into an open top box.

Conditions—We must fold along dotted lines only.

Goal —Determine which figures fold into an open top box and which do not.

Design a Solution Strategy

Cut out all twelve figures or copy them onto graph paper and cut them out. See which figures fold into an open top box. Make a list of the results.

Carry Out Plan

Of the twelve figures, only 1, 3, 4, 5, 8, 9, and 11 fold into an open-top box. It is impossible to fold the other configurations into a box.

Fold Into Open Top Box	Impossible
1, 3, 4, 5, 8, 9, 11	2, 6, 7, 10, 12

Evaluate Results

This problem can be attacked in two ways. The strategy above works from the *given* information to the *goal*. We could just as easily cut the tops off several small milk cartons and see which figures can be made by cutting along the edges of the box and laying it flat. Here we are beginning with the *goal* and working backward to the *given* figures. In either case, exactly seven different configurations will be found.

Note: The two figures below are considered to be the same. If we flip one over, it matches exactly with the other.

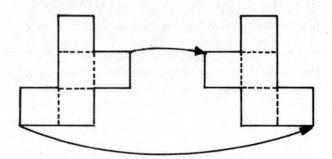

The twelve figures used here are called pentominoes. Your class will enjoy the wide range of puzzles and activities which make use of these pieces. If you add one extra 2 × 2 square to give a total of thirteen pieces,

it is possible to make an 8 × 8 square using all thirteen pieces with no overlapping or empty squares. There are many solutions to this puzzle; see if your class can find just one! The following puzzle has been started for you.

Pentomino Puzzle

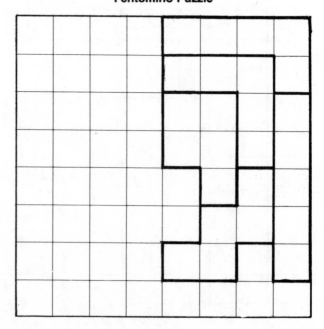

WHAT'S THE DIFFERENCE?

(Problem Starter Sheet 13, page 115)

Pick any four numbers and write them in a square, as below.

4   8

7   1

Next, connect any two numbers without going across the middle. Find the difference between the two number values and write it at the center of the line.

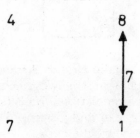

Do the same with the other pairs.

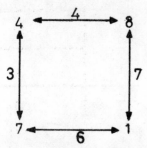

Now connect these numbers with lines and find their differences.

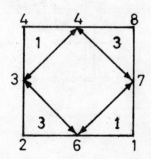

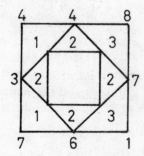

This time all the answers are the same.
Will this always happen for any four starting numbers?
Will you always end up with 2 for a final answer?
What happens if you start with bigger numbers?

This problem needed three steps to get to a common difference. Can you find four numbers that need four steps? Five steps? Six steps?

SOLUTION:
WHAT'S THE DIFFERENCE?

Understand the Problem

Facts —Four numbers are placed on the corners of a square.

—Differences are found for each pair of adjacent numbers.

—These four numbers are again connected in a square array and the difference found as before. The process is continued until you arrive at a common answer.

Conditions—Always compute the positive difference between two numbers. For example, the difference between 3 and 5 is 2, not −2.

Goal —Find out if you end at a common difference for any four numbers. Does this final answer vary? Can you find four numbers that require four steps to arrive at a common difference? Five steps? Six steps?

Design a Solution Strategy

Try many combinations of four numbers. Record the original numbers and the number of steps it takes you to reach a common difference and the final answer.

Carry Out Plan

The table below lists the results of several experiments:

4 Numbers	Number of Steps	Common Difference
4, 8, 1, 7	3	2
3, 88, 99, 57	3	27
1, 2, 8, 4	5	2
1, 2, 4, 8	6	2
1, 3, 9, 27	5	8
12, 77, 2, 25	3	42
2, 5, 7, 1	4	2
3, 6, 9, 12	1	3
15, 8, 11, 4	2	4

Evaluate Results

Every example seems to arrive eventually at a common difference. The final answer varies and the number of steps ranges from one to six. We have been unable to find an example that requires more than six steps to arrive at a common difference. Perhaps your class can find a set of four numbers that requires more than six steps.

An interesting extension of this problem involves rearranging the order of a set of numbers and observing the required number of differences to arrive at a common answer. (See [1, 2, 8, 4] and [1, 2, 4, 8] above). The final difference seems to be the same but the number of steps varies. Is this the case for other sets of numbers? A calculator may help with this one.

Problem and Solution 14

GOLD DIGGERS

(Problem Starter Sheet 14, page 116)

Digger Jenkins was a gold assayer who flew all over Alaska in a rickety little plane weighing ore for eager prospectors. His job was to weigh samples very accurately, but he also had to be careful not to overload his tiny plane with equipment. To measure, he packed only three mass pieces—1 gram, 3 gram and 9 gram weights. For example, he could weigh a 4-gram sample of gold ore like this:

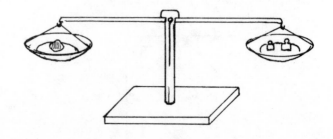

Digger claimed he could weigh any amount of ore from 1 to 13 grams. (No fractions, of course.) Is Digger right?

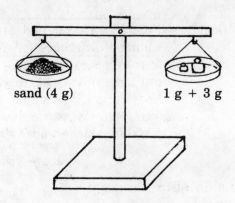

sand (4 g)   1 g + 3 g

SOLUTION: GOLD DIGGERS

Understand the Problem

Facts —You must use a pan balance and three mass pieces—1, 3, and 9 grams.

—You can put one or more pieces of mass on either pan.

Conditions—You can only weigh to the nearest whole gram.

Goal —How many different weights can be measured using only 1, 3 and 9 gram mass pieces?

Design Solution Strategy

Using a pan balance and three mass pieces, weigh out several piles of sand or rice. Record the results in a table.

Carry Out Plan

Conduct a few experiments with the pan balance.

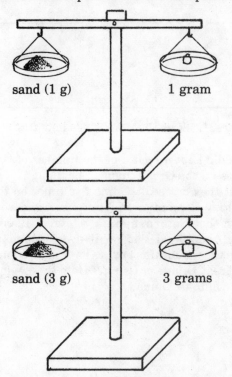

sand (1 g)   1 gram

sand (3 g)   3 grams

The key to weighing two and five grams of sand is to realize that by placing mass pieces on both pans, you actually subtract (counterbalance) the mass of the small weight from the larger. It may be possible for some children to complete the table without actually carrying out all the weighings.

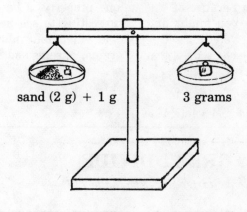

sand (2 g) + 1 g   3 grams

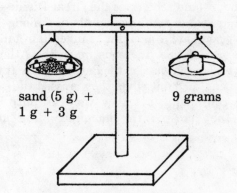

sand (5 g) + 1 g + 3 g   9 grams

63

Mass of Sand (grams)	Left Pan	Right Pan
1	sand	1 gram
2	sand + 1 gram m.p.	3 gram m.p.
3	sand	3 gram m.p.
4	sand	1 gram m.p. + 3 gram m.p.
5	sand + 1 gram m.p. + 3 gram m.p.	9 gram m.p.
6	sand + 3 gram m.p.	9 gram m.p.
7	sand + 3 gram m.p.	1 gram m.p. + 9 gram m.p.
8	sand + 1 gram m.p.	9 gram m.p.
9	sand	9 gram m.p.
10	sand	1 gram m.p. + 9 gram m.p.
11	sand + 1 gram m.p.	3 gram + 9 gram m.p.
12	sand	3 gram m.p. + 9 gram m.p.
13	sand	1 gram m.p. + 3 gram m.p. + 9 gram m.p.

(m.p. = mass piece)

Evaluate Results

It is in fact possible for Digger to weigh piles of ore from 1 to 13 grams in mass. It is rather remarkable that these three mass pieces allow such a large number of weighings. These pieces were chosen because of this unique property of base-three. You might find it interesting to see how many weighings are possible when four mass pieces are used—1 gram, 3 grams, 9 grams and 27 grams. The results are quite surprising. Base-two mass pieces (1, 2, 4, 8, 16, 32, etc.) offer similar weighing properties though more mass pieces are needed. Base-two mass pieces have the added advantage of requiring placement only on the right hand pan. Try other bases (4, 5, 10) to see which requires the fewest mass pieces to measure any whole number mass.

Problem and Solution 15

THE GREAT DIVIDE

(Problem Starter Sheet 15, page 117)

Otto Levique and his family were taking a trip across Canada by car. When they came to the Rocky Mountains, his daughter, Michelle, who had been studying geography in school, explained that they would soon cross the Great Divide—an imaginary line running lengthwise along the highest points of a mountain range. Rain falling to the east of this line ends up in the Atlantic Ocean and to the west, in the Pacific Ocean. It was an exciting moment when they crossed the "roof of the continent," but they were all surprised when they crossed the imaginary line more than once. Look at the map to see how this could happen.

Michelle kept a record of the number of times they crossed the Great Divide. She thought it was odd that they crossed the line five times on their route from Edmonton to Vancouver and seven times on their return, making a total of 12 crossings for the round trip. Will every round trip through the mountains always have an even number of Great Divide crossings? Help the Leviques with the auto-dilemma.

64

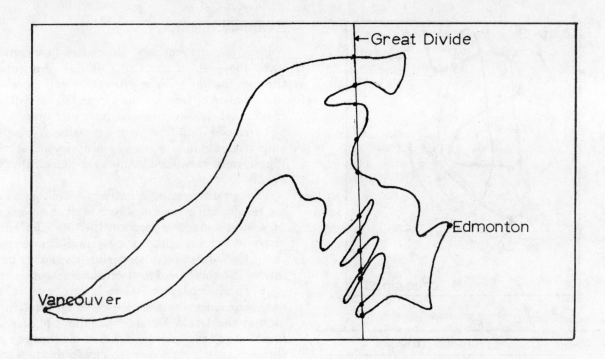

SOLUTION: THE GREAT DIVIDE

Understand the Problem

Facts —The Great Divide is an imaginary line connecting the highest points, lengthwise, along a mountain range.

—The road weaves back and forth across the line as it works its way through the mountains.

Conditions—You must make a round trip from Edmonton to Vancouver to Edmonton.

—You cannot go around mountains, through the Panama Canal, or across the Arctic.

Goal —Find out if you must always cross the Great Divide an even number of times when making a round trip.

Design a Solution Strategy

Draw a map and conduct several experiments. Organize the data in a table and look for patterns.

Carry Out Plan

The following maps show several configurations of routes and Great Divides. The results of these two routes along with others are summarized in the table below.

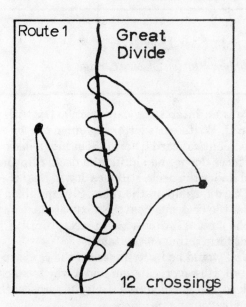

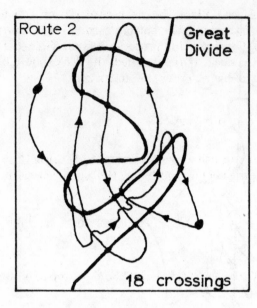

Route 2
Great Divide
18 crossings

Route	Number of Crossings		
	Going	Returning	Total
1	9	3	12
2	13	5	18
3	1	1	2
4	3	1	4
5			
6			

Problem and Solution 16

Evaluate Results

A clear pattern emerges. No matter how convoluted the path of the Great Divide, any route through the range in one direction will cross an odd number of times. (The Great Divide cannot cross itself, however.) A round trip requires an odd-plus-odd (even) number of crossings. You and your students may want to justify to yourselves that the sum of two odd numbers is, in fact, always even.

Though discovering a pattern doesn't guarantee that it will work for all cases, at the elementary level deductive proofs (which do offer such guarantees) may not be appropriate. If everyone in the class does several experiments and the pattern holds, this "proof by desire" seems sufficient.

As an alternative solution, it is interesting to note that since you can not make an "end run" around the Great Divide line, the situation is identical to counting the number of times you go through your front door each day from when you get out of bed until you return at night. There is a tradition in rural New England which says that the greatest comfort in life is living in the house you were born in. The only way in which you can sit in any house having the comfort of knowing that you have passed through the door an even number of times is to have been born there. All others present will have passed through an odd number of times.

Stack the Deck
(Problem Starter Sheet 16, page 118)

Here is an interesting card trick to try with your friends. Write each letter of your name on separate, identical cards. Form them into a deck with the faces down and shuffle the deck. Slip the top card under the deck, still face down. Deal the second card face up on the table. Slip the third card under the deck and deal the next card face up next to the first. Continue this process until all the cards form a line on the table.

You would be lucky indeed if the cards spelled a word. However, can you find a way to stack the deck so that when you deal out the cards as above, it spells your name?

If you can figure out a solution, it's fun to surprise your friends by using their names.

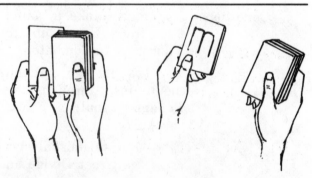

Slip one card under deck.

Deal next card face up.

SOLUTION: STACK THE DECK

Understand the Problem

Facts—Each letter of a name is written on separate, identical cards.

—The cards are dealt one at a time. You slip the first card under the deck, place the second card face up on the table, slip the third card under the deck, place the next card face up, and so on.

—Stop when all cards are on the table.

Conditions—Cards should be placed next to each other on the table from left to right. *Note:* It is possible to spell out the names backwards to heighten the element of surprise.

Goal—Arrange the deck so that when it is dealt out in the above manner, the cards will spell out a name.

Design a Solution Strategy

Try working the problem backwards by first spelling out the name on the table, then reversing the dealing procedure until you have a completed deck. If the name is long, try a shorter one for practice. It might be helpful also to use numbered cards instead of letters. Use the same strategy, only begin with a series of cards numbered from one to ten. Playing cards work well.

Carry Out Plan

Begin with the cards arranged on the table as in the example below.

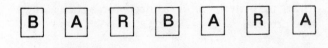

Pick up the last card (A) and place it on top of the deck. (The deck has zero cards at the beginning.) Slip the bottom card on the top, face down. (The bottom card is the top card in this case so nothing

changes.) Place the next card (R) on top (face down) and slip the bottom card (A) face down on top. Continue this process until all the cards are in the deck. When finished, the deck should be in the following order (top to bottom).

B B R A A R A

If you use a series of numbered cards (1 to 10) begin as below and follow the same procedure.

| 1 | 2 | 3 | 4 | 5 | 6 | 7 | 8 | 9 | 10 |

The order of the deck should be (top to bottom):

8, 1, 6, 2, 10, 3, 7, 4, 9, 5

Evaluate Results

Reverse the process and the deck should "spell" the name or number sequence correctly. Any sequence of letters or numbers can be arranged into a deck in this manner.

It is interesting to compare this problem to "Clyde the Class Clown" (Problem Solution Sheet 32). If you simply arrange the deck of number cards from 1 to 10 (1 on top and 10 on bottom) and deal them out as described above, the last card will tell you the "lucky" position for a class of ten.

Some additional problems which might challenge your class include arranging the deck to:

1. Spell their first and last names.

2. Spell their names backwards.

3. Count down from 10 to 1.

4. Write a friend's telephone number.

5. Spell out a funny saying.

6. Spell out a secret message.

7. Spell out their names but slip two cards under the deck each time instead of one.

FOUR ACES

(Problem Starter Sheet 17, page 119)

This simple card trick sounds complicated but it is actually very easy to do.

1. Using an ordinary deck of cards cut the cards into four roughly equal piles and lay them out next to each other in front of you.

2. Pick up the pile that came from the bottom of the deck (pile 4), and deal three cards face down on the table in the same spot where the pile was.

3. Deal one card from pile 4 face down on top of each of the other three decks and place the pile back where it came from, on top of the three cards.

4. Repeat the process with the other three piles, ending with the pile that was on top of the original deck (pile 1).

5. Turning over the top card on each pile gives a surprising result—4 aces!

Deck   1   2   3   4
        Top of   Bottom
        deck   of deck

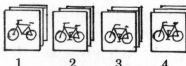

1   2   3   4

- Pick up pile 4
- Deal 3 cards down
- Deal 1 card on piles 1, 2 and 3
- Replace pile 4
- Repeat process with 1, 2 and 3

Can you figure out how the trick works?

SOLUTION: FOUR ACES

Understand the Problem

Facts   —You use a regular deck of cards.

        —Cut the deck into four piles with the top pile on the left (pile 1) and bottom pile on the right (pile 4). Pick up the bottom pile (4), deal three cards down in same spot where pile 4 was, then deal one card face down on each of the other piles. Repeat with other piles, ending with pile 1.

        —Turning over the top card on each deck exposes the four aces.

Conditions—Cards in the original deck must be prearranged to exorcise the magic.

Goal   —Find out how the original deck was arranged in order to explain the magic.

Design a Solution Strategy

Work the problem backwards, keeping track of the four aces to see how to stack the original deck.

Carry Out Plan

Starting with the final result, reverse each step in the process.

1   2   3   4

1. Turn the aces face down on top of the four piles.

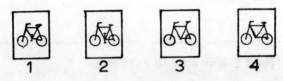

2. Pick up the top card on each pile and put them on top of pile 1.

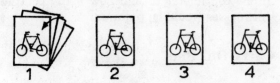

Note. The four aces are now on top of pile 1.

3. Pick up pile 1. Put the bottom three cards on top of the pile.

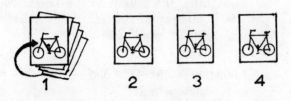

Note. The aces in pile 1 are now under three cards.

4. Pick up pile 2. Place one card from the top of piles 1, 3, and 4 on pile 2. Move bottom three cards to top of pile 2 and replace the pile in its original position. Aces still in pile 1 are now under two cards.

5. Repeat this process two more times using piles 3 and 4. Aces in pile 1 are now on top of the pile.

6. Pick up the four piles in order with 1 on the top and 4 on the bottom.

Evaluate Results

To set up the deck for the trick simply place four aces on top of the deck. The rest of the trick works automatically. All the moving around of cards and piles is simply to confuse the observers. Like most card tricks, if your audience knew how simple it was, they would be quite upset with themselves.

As you may have noticed, you can change the order in which the piles are picked up, except pile #1 must be used last. Many card tricks of this type can be invented by your students, offering an excellent opportunity for them to develop their organizational skills and short term memory.

STACK 'EM HIGH

(Problem Starter Sheet 18, page 120)

Suzanne Megapenny is very rich. She got a bit bored one day and told her banker to immediately deliver one million new one dollar bills to her house. She sat in her living room and began to stack the bills on top of each other in a single column. How high will the stack be?

SOLUTION: STACK 'EM HIGH

Understand the Problem

Facts	—Megapenny has one million new one dollar bills.
	—She is making a single stack of bills, each bill on top of the other.
Conditions	—Assume a dollar bill is about the same thickness as a book page.
	—Since the bills are new, you don't need to consider wrinkles.
Goal	—Estimate the height of the stack of one million dollar bills.

Design a Solution Strategy

Estimate the number of dollar bills in a stack one centimeter thick by measuring a one centimeter thickness on the edge of a book and counting the pages. Divide one million by the number of pages in one centimeter to find how many centimeter thicknesses would be required.

Carry Out Plan

Measure a one centimeter thickness across the end of a book. Count the pages to find out the approximate number of dollars in a 1 cm thick stack. A short cut to counting is to open any book to page 1 and measure a depth of 1 cm. Dividing the last page number in the stack by 2 gives you the total number of pages. Can your class figure out why?

Let's say there are 80 pages per centimeter. Dividing 1,000,000 by 80 gives the number of centimeter stacks needed. For example, if I had 250 one dollar bills, the height of the stack would equal 250 ÷ 80 or approximately 3 cm. Therefore, one million dollars would stack up:

$$1,000,000 \div 80 = 125,000 \text{ cm}$$
or 125 meters high!

Evaluate Results

To get an idea of how tall this is, remember a room is about 3 meters high. Megapenny's living room would have to be over 40 stories high to hold all that wealth.

COUNT ON

(Problem Starter Sheet 19, page 121)

One rainy afternoon Tara couldn't find anyone to play with so she decided to count to a billion. Can you find out about how long it would take Tara to finish? One hour? Two hours? All day? How old are you in seconds?

SOLUTION: COUNT ON

Understanding the Problem

Facts —Use natural numbers (1, 2, 3, 4, 5, . . .).

Conditions—Count steady at a rate of one number a second.

Goal —Find how long it will take Tara to count to one billion.

Design a Solution Strategy

For simplicity, let's estimate that it takes one second to count each number. Using a calculator, figure out how high Tara could count in an hour, a day, a week, and a year. Organize the results in a table.

Carry Out Plan

The following table lists how high you could count in a second, minute, hour, day, etc., if you count one number each second.

Time	Count
1 second	1
1 minute	60
1 hour	3600
1 day	86,400
1 week	604,800
1 year	31,449,600
10 years	314,496,000 (most calculators "give up" here and overflow.)
30 years	943,488,000 (almost there.)
32 years	1,006,387,200 (we made it!)

Evaluate Results

This problem clearly demonstrates the limitations of the simple hand-held calculator. The largest number most calculators can show accurately is 99,999,999, far smaller than our goal. In fact, we can calculate only a little more than three years worth of counting. A bit of "old fashioned" arithmetic quickly shows that Tara would have to count day and night for over thirty-one years to reach her goal! It would certainly be a long rainy afternoon.

Using the table it is easy to figure your age in seconds. Anyone older than three years will have to figure it out by hand, however, unless they have a very fancy calculator. As of October 3, 1980 the author was exactly 1,037,836,800 seconds old. Can you figure out his birthday and age?

GRAINS OF RICE

(Problem Starter Sheet 20, page 122)

How many grains of rice are in a bag of rice? One hundred grains? One thousand grains? One million grains?

To find out you need

A bag of rice

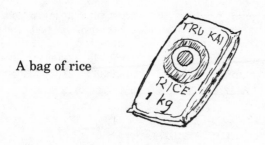

A pan-balance scale

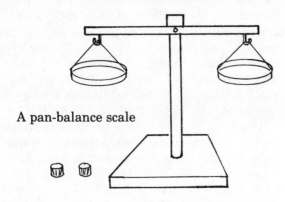

A calculator

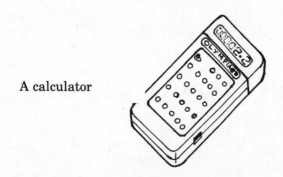

SOLUTION: GRAINS OF RICE

Understand the Problem

Facts —A bag of rice contains many grains.

—The grains are about the same size.

—Two common sizes are 1 kilogram and 1 pound bags.

Conditions—You have access to only a pan balance, small cups, and a calculator.

Goal —Find the approximate number of grains in a bag of rice.

Design a Solution Strategy

Measure out one small cup of rice. Any small coffee-creamer size cups will work. Count the grains. For younger children, a team approach to this counting task may be in order. Using the balance, weigh out quantities of rice one cup at a time to find the total number of cups in a bag. This process can be speeded up considerably by first measuring out one cup on each side of the balance. Next, place both measured cups on the same pan and pour rice on the other pan until it balances. Again put the two piles together on one pan (now four cups) and weigh out an equivalent amount on the balance. Continuing this process of doubling (1, 2, 8, 16 ... cups), one is able to quickly determine the number of cups in the bag. Using a calculator, multiply the number of grains in *one* cup by the total number of cups to find the total number of grains in the bag.

Carry Out Plan

The number of grains in a coffee-creamer cup is about 1135. A kilogram bag of rice contains approximately 38 creamer-cups of rice. The total number of grains is $38 \times 1135 = 43,130$ grains.

Evaluate Results

The answer above is only approximate. Its accuracy depends on the consistency in grain size and accuracy in measurement. Obviously there will be errors; however, the answer does give a reasonable approximation to the number of grains.

The size of the measuring cup isn't important, though a small one simplifies the counting process and minimizes error due to a fractional part of a cup left over when weighing out the whole bag.

An interesting extension to this problem for older children is to consider how large a packing crate would be required to contain 1 million grains of rice. You might even want to set your class to work finding the number of grains of rice it would take to fill your classroom. Would a billion grains do it? How many grains of rice in one serving? How many people would it take to eat a room full of rice?

Problem and Solution 21

MONEY MATTERS

(Problem Starter Sheet 21, page 123)

One day, Rosa decided to play a trick on her brother, Aaron. She said, "I have 21¢ in my pocket. If you can tell me all the possible combinations of pennies, nickels and dimes which make up 21¢, I'll buy you an ice cream cone." Here is one way:

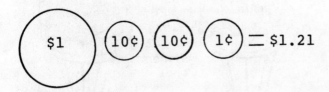

After Aaron started making his list Rosa said, "I just found a dollar in my other pocket. If you can find all the ways to make change for $1.21 I'll buy you a double-dipper cone. You can use pennies, nickels, dimes, quarters, half dollars and a silver dollar." Here is one way:

Can you help Aaron find all the ways to make change for 21¢? For $1.21?

SOLUTION: MONEY MATTERS

Understanding the Problem

Facts —First Rosa had 21¢ in her pocket, then she had $1.21 in her pocket.

—You can use 1¢, 5¢, 10¢, 25¢, 50¢, and $1 coins.

Conditions—You can use as many coins as necessary.

—You are not required to use all six coins at once.

Goal —List all possible combinations of coins equaling 21¢ and $1.21.

Design a Solution Strategy

Construct a list of combinations of one or more coins which equal 21¢. Begin with the largest possible coin and list all possible combinations with smaller coins. Systematically reduce the size of the initial coin until you reach 21 pennies. Try the same task for $1.21.

Carry Out Plan

The table below lists all the combinations of pennies, nickels, and dimes adding up to 21¢. The key to the solution is being systematic in listing the combinations so you will know when you are finished.

Change for 21¢

	10¢	5¢	1¢
1	2	0	1
2	1	2	1
3	1	1	6
4	1	0	11
5	0	4	1
6	0	3	6
7	0	2	11
8	0	1	16
9	0	0	21

Evaluate Results

There are exactly nine ways to make change for 21¢. Aaron should have no problem collecting his first scoop of ice cream. Trying a similar procedure for $1.21, however, presents a surprisingly complex situation. We now have to keep track of six types of coins (pennies, nickels, dimes, quarters, half dollars, and dollars). The number of combinations grows distressingly fast, trying the patience of even the most loving brother. If you or your students try to solve this one, you can at least have satisfaction in knowing that the author stayed up late into the night completing the table. Aaron would have to work hard indeed for that double dipper, since there are 782 ways to make change for $1.21!

Problem and Solution 22

ICE-CREAM EXPERT

(Problem Starter Sheet 22, page 124)

Bud was an expert ice-cream eater. He could name any flavor blindfolded. When he bought an ice cream cone not only did he choose the flavors carefully, but he had to have them stacked on the cone in the right order. Strawberry on top with vanilla on the bottom was for hot days. Vanilla on top and strawberry on the bottom helped him to think better.

There are only two ways of building a cone with two flavors. (You must use both flavors.) How many different cones could Bud order with three flavors? Four flavors? Five flavors?

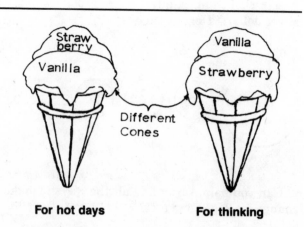

For hot days   For thinking

SOLUTION: ICE CREAM

Understand the Problem

Facts —Ice-cream scoops stack one on top of the other.

—Ice-cream scoops stacked in various orders are considered different.

Condition —You must use all the chosen flavors on each cone.

Goal —Find the number of different cones which can be made from three, four and five flavors.

Design a Solution Strategy

Develop a table of different cones starting with one flavor, then two and so on. Construct the list in a systematic manner to insure that no possibilities are skipped. Count the total number of cones (called permutations) and try to discover a pattern involving the number of flavors and the number of cones.

Carry Out Plan

The table below lists all the permutations of scoops for one through four flavors.

Number of Different Cones
(Must use all flavors.)

S – Strawberry
V – Vanilla
C – Chocolate
P – Pecan

Flavors	Combinations	Total Cones
1		1
2		2
3		6
4		24

Evaluate Results

Notice that the list is "growing" very quickly. Many times when solving a problem, it is useful to look for a pattern in order to reduce the amount of labor. Some problems get so complicated that you must find a logical or arithmetical shortcut in order to finish in a reasonable amount of time. Such is the case with the current problem. Observe the following table:

Number of Flavors	Number of Cones
1	1
2	2
3	6
4	24
5	?

Notice that to find the number of permutations of, say, three flavors, simply multiply 3 by the number of cones for two flavors:

$$3 \times 2 = 6$$

Does this pattern always hold?

$$2 \times 1 = 2$$
$$3 \times 2 = 6$$
$$4 \times 6 = 24$$
$$5 \times 24 = 120$$

Notice that if the pattern holds, the number of possible cones using five flavors is 120! Consider how permutations grow. By adding an additional flavor you are simply taking the previous set of cones (say six cones for three flavors) and giving each of the four flavors a chance to be on top (4 × 6 = 24). The table can be continued as below:

Number of Flavors	Number of Cones
1	1
2	2
3	6
4	24
5	120
6	720
7	5040
8	40,320

It is interesting to note that this pattern actually describes the process of multiplying together all the natural numbers up to and including the number of flavors considered. For example, with five flavors there are:

$$1 \times 2 \times 3 \times 4 \times 5 = 120 \text{ cones}$$

Mathematicians call this process "factorial." We use the notation below to indicate the factorial function.

$$5! = 120$$

It should be easy to determine the number of permutations for various numbers of flavors. Have your students find out the largest factorial their calculator can swallow.

Problem and Solution 23

HAMBURGER HEAVEN
(Problem Starter Sheet 23, page 125)

Hamburger Heaven

	Menu	
Burgers	*Fries 'n Rings*	*Drinks*
1. Boring Burger ....30¢	1. French Fries ....45¢	1. Orange ....30¢
2. Kiloburger ....75¢	2. Onion Rings ....65¢	2. Coke ....30¢
3. Fat Mac $1.50		3. Root Beer ....30¢
		4. Milk ....55¢

If you could pick one item from each column, how many different meals could you make? Here are two different meals:

1. Fat Mac, Onion Rings, Root Beer
2. Fat Mac, French Fries, Milk

How many meals would be possible if one more type of hamburger was added to the menu?

SOLUTION: HAMBURGER HEAVEN

Understand the Problem

Facts —There are three types of hamburgers, two types of fries, and four types of drinks.

Conditions—Must choose one item from each column to be called a meal.

—A meal is "different" if one item changed.

Goal —Find how many different meals can be constructed from Hamburger Heaven's menu.

Design a Solution Strategy

Develop a list of possible meals using a systematic process so no combination will be overlooked. Abbreviating the food names might simplify the listing process.

Carry Out Plan

The following list was formed by selecting the first item in each row. We then changed only the drink, giving us the first four meals. Next we changed the french fries (FF) to onion rings (OR) and repeated the process, giving four more meals. We then changed to the second burger and repeated from the start, giving eight more meals. The process was systematically continued until all possible combinations were listed.

List of Meals

Meal	Hamburger	Fry	Drink
1	BB (Boring Burger)	FF (French Fry)	OG (Orange)
2	BB	FF	CK (Coke)
3	BB	FF	RB (Root Beer)
4	BB	FF	ML (Milk)
5	BB	OR (Onion Rings)	OG
6	BB	OR	CK
7	BB	OR	RB
8	BB	OR	ML
9	KB (Kiloburger)	FF	OG
10	KB	FF	CK
11	KB	FF	RB
12	KB	FF	ML
13	KB	OR	OG
14	KB	OR	CK
15	KB	OR	RB
16	KB	OR	ML
17	FM (Fat Mac)	FF	OG
18	FM	FF	CK
19	FM	FF	RB
20	FM	FF	ML
21	FM	OR	OG
22	FM	OR	CK
23	FM	OR	RB
24	FM	OR	ML

Evaluate Results

It would be possible to eat twenty-four days in a row at Hamburger Heaven and never eat the same meal twice—UGH! This type of combination problem applies to many of our everyday activities. When we get dressed in the morning we choose from a limited number of items, yet even a modest wardrobe offers a huge number of possible combinations.

The final question in the problem leads to a more important discovery. If we added one more burger, how many additional meals could we construct? Observing our list above, notice that each burger is included in eight meals. One more burger should add a similar number. Looking a bit further, if we include an additional fry (extra greasy) we add twelve meals. One extra drink increases the number of meals by only six.

One final observation is perhaps the most surprising. Notice that the total number of combinations is equal to the product of the number of items in each column. In this case:

$$\text{Original menu} - 3 \times 2 \times 4 = 24$$

This explains how the number of meals grows.

Add one burger—$4 \times 2 \times 4 = 32$
(adds 8 meals)
Add one fry—$3 \times 3 \times 4 = 36$
(adds 12 meals)
Add one drink—$3 \times 2 \times 5 = 30$
(adds 6 meals)

Does this pattern always work? What happens when a fourth column (dessert) is included? Set your class to work on extending their understanding of combinations. They will eat it up! (See "Ice-Cream Expert," page 74.)

Problem and Solution 24

POPCORN TRUTH

(Problem Starter Sheet 24, page 126)

Companies are always advertising that their product is better than the rest. "Our toothpaste makes your teeth whiter"; "Kids eat more Corn Puffies than any other cereal." Ever wonder if the commercials are true? Here is an ad for you to test out for yourself: "You pay a little more, but our popcorn leaves fewer unpopped kernels, so it's a better buy."

Go to the store and buy the same size bag of the *most* expensive and *least* expensive popcorn. Do an experiment to find out if the expensive popcorn is actually a better buy.

SOLUTION: POPCORN TRUTH

Understand the Problem

Facts —We have two brands of popcorn.
—Brand X costs more than Brand Y.

Conditions—Brand X is supposed to pop more completely than Brand Y.

Goal —Find if Brand X is a better buy than Brand Y.

Design a Solution Strategy

Count out 250 kernels of Brand X and Y. Pop each brand separately in the same popper for the same amount of time. Count the number of unpopped kernels and record in a table. Compare the difference in popping efficiency to the initial cost.

Carry Out Plan

This experiment could be carried out in school or at home. A sufficient supply of Brand X and Y popcorn should be provided so students can work in pairs or in small groups. The activity works best in a classroom when set up as a learning center and made available throughout the day.

Since each region of the country will have different brands of popcorn to investigate, the following is offered as an example only. Suppose we bought two bags of popcorn:

Popcorn	Cost
Brand X—250 grams	$1.40
Brand Y—250 grams	$1.00

Popping 250 kernels of each brand for four minutes gave the following results. (We warmed up the popper before putting in the corn for each experiment.)

Popping Results

	Number of Kernels	Number of Remaining Kernels	Failure Rate
Brand X	250	8	3.2%
Brand Y	250	37	14.8%

Out of 250 kernels, Brand X had 8 remaining and Brand Y had 37 remaining. The percent failure is the number remaining divided by the total number of kernels. For example, if 1 out of 100 kernels didn't pop, the failure rate would be:

$$1 \div 100 = .01 \text{ or } 1\%$$

Students should be encouraged to use a calculator to carry out these computations.

Evaluate Results

Certainly the expensive Brand X has a lower failure rate (3.2%) as compared to Brand Y (14.8%). But are the rates different enough to compensate for the higher initial price?

First let's determine how much "poppable" corn we actually purchased. Out of 250 grams, if we assume the failure rates above are reasonably accurate, only part of the corn we bought is eatable.

Original Amount	Failure Rate	Unpoppable	Eatable Corn
Brand X 250 grams	3.2%	8 grams	242 grams
Brand Y 250 grams	14.8%	37 grams	213 grams

So of the amount purchased, only 242 grams of Brand X and 213 grams of Brand Y are eatable. To determine the actual cost per gram of eatable corn, we divide the total price by the number of grams. For example, if 10 cents buys 5 grams, each gram costs 2 cents ($10 \div 5 = 2$). Therefore:

	Total Cost	Eatable Amount	Price/Gram
Brand X	$1.40	242 grams	$.0057
Brand Y	$1.00	213 grams	$.0046

Even with a lower failure rate, Brand X costs about a tenth of a cent more per gram than Brand Y. (Note that $.0057 is a bit more than ½ cent, .0046 is a bit less than ½ cent.) In fact, even if Brand X had a zero failure rate (all the kernels popped) the failure rate for Brand Y would have to double (28%) before it would become more "expensive."

Other consumer oriented experiments can be designed to test claims about paper towels, liquid detergent and hand soaps. Problem solving in the marketplace can become a valuable skill.

COW THOUGHTS

(Problem Starter Sheet 25, page 127)

Pico Steerman, a well-known rancher, invented a new style corral for his cattle. By driving a herd of steers through gate *A,* the cow-doctor could check them one at a time for disease at station *B.*

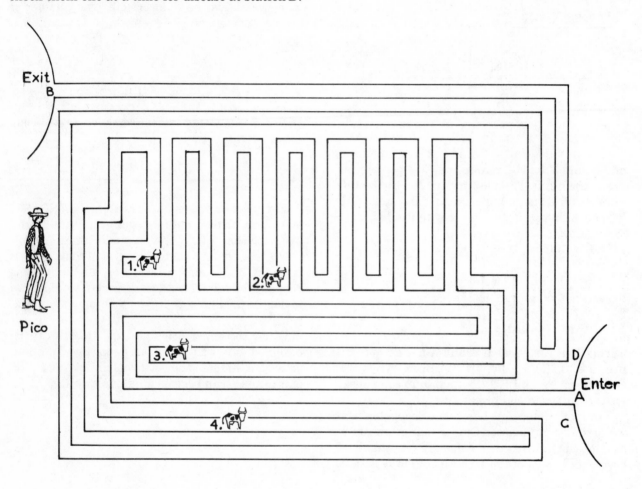

Sometimes a stray cow wanders into the maze through the opening at *C* or *D,* and though it appears to be trapped in the corral, it is actually free. Help Pico, who is standing outside the corral, figure out a way to quickly determine which steers are inside the corral and which are free to roam the range. Can you figure out a method that will always work, regardless of the position of the cow or how complex the maze? Remember, Pico can't look down on the corral, as shown in the picture above.

SOLUTION: COW THOUGHTS

Understand the Problem

Facts —Cows are either inside or outside the corral.

Conditions—The corral must be one region (i.e., one corral), or cows couldn't go completely through to exit.

—An observer on the outside must be able to determine whether a cow is *inside* or *free* without being able to test possible paths to freedom (you would need a helicopter so you could look down from above).

Goal —Find a quick method to determine if a cow is safely inside the corral or is free.

Design a Solution Strategy

Simplify the problem situation by starting with a very simple corral. If you imagine yourself standing outside looking at a cow inside, how many fences are between you and the cow? Try the same procedure with the cow outside. Continue this process with more and more complicated corrals, organize the results in a table, and look for a pattern.

Carry Out Plan

Start with a simple corral.

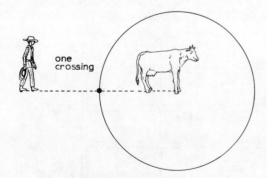

There is always exactly one fence between you and the cow if the cow is inside.

If the cow is outside, there can be either zero or two fences between you and the cow.

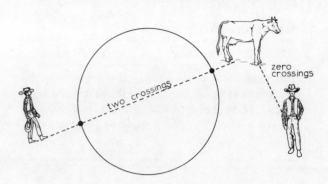

Note. If your line of sight falls along the edge of the fence and you don't know whether to count it as zero, one or two crossings, move a bit to one side until the situation becomes clear.

A slightly more complicated corral adds more information to the situation.

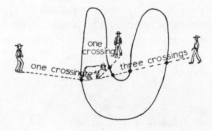

If the cow is inside there is either one or three fence crossings. If the cow is outside there is zero, two, or four crossings.

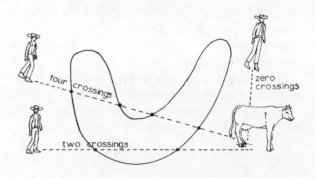

These and the results of several other experiments are organized in the table below. Search for patterns.

Number of Fence Crossings

Corral	Cow Inside	Cow Outside
1	1	0 or 2
2	1 or 3	0 or 2 or 4
3	1, 3 or 5	0 or 2 or 4 or 6
4	1 or 3 or 5 or 7	0 or 2 or 4 or 6 or 8
5		

Evaluate Results

A clear pattern emerges in the table above. If the cow is inside, there seems to be an odd number of fences between the observer and the cow. If outside, an even number of fence crossings will be noted. Therefore, in Pico's corral, cows 1 and 3 are outside, 2 and 4 inside.

We can help Pico solve his problem by suggesting that he simply count the number of fences between himself and any cow of interest. If there are an odd number of crossings he has nothing to worry about. However, if the number turns up even, Pico has a loose cow on his hands.

An interesting magic trick can be performed based on this same principle. You need a piece of string approximately 2 meters long. Tie the ends of the string together to form a long loop. On a smooth table, place your finger inside the loop and pull it into a complicated, snake-like pattern. Make sure the string doesn't cross over itself anywhere. Remember the spot where your finger was when you constructed the string maze. Now have an observer place a finger anywhere inside the pattern. You instantly report whether the finger is inside or outside the loop. When pulled his finger will either be caught or the loop will neatly slip away.

The trick is to quickly count the number of string crossings between the observer's finger and the spot where your finger was when you completed the loop pattern. If the number is even, the observer's finger will be caught; if odd, it will be outside the loop. An even more dramatic exercise involves your carefully placing all five fingers of the observer's hand in such a way that there are exactly two strings between each finger. When the loop is pulled, all five fingers will either be caught or the loop will pull cleanly away. Such magic!

Problem and Solution 26

CLASSROOM MANEUVERS
(Problem Starter Sheet 26, page 128)

Mr. Nitpicker's classroom is organized in five neat rows with five desks in each row. The desks are separated so you can walk in front and behind, as well as between them.

Arthur and the teacher are standing as in the picture. What is the shortest route for Arthur to walk in order to ask Mr. Nitpicker for the hall pass?

Arthur

Mr Nitpicker

Here are two possible routes:

Walks 10 units

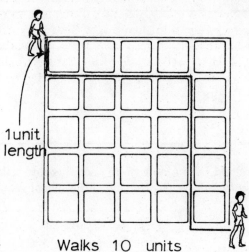

1unit
length

Walks 10 units

SOLUTION:
CLASSROOM MANEUVERS

Understand the Problem

Facts — There are five rows of desks with five in each row.

— The desks are evenly spaced so you can walk in front, behind, and between them.

— Arthur and the teacher are on opposite corners of the classroom.

Conditions — Arthur must walk between desks (no jumping over).

— The desks must be close enough together so that you must make sharp turns.

Goal — Find the shortest route from Arthur to Mr. Nitpicker.

Design a Solution Strategy

Using centimeter-squared paper, make several five-unit squares. Using these simplified model sketches, conduct several experiments and record the route lengths. Look for a pattern.

Carry Out Plan

Here are several different routes:

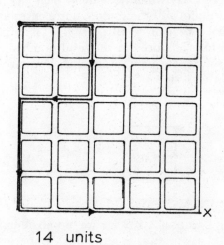

14 units

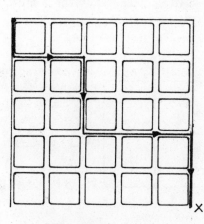

10 units

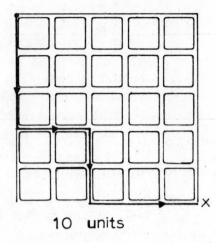

10 units

Evaluate Results

Careful observation of the sketches above should show that as long as Arthur moves to the right and towards the front, he will always walk exactly ten units. Only when he doubles back (as in the first example) will the route require extra steps.

As an extension to this problem, it might be interesting to figure out the total number of different ten-unit routes. Start with a square with one unit on a side:

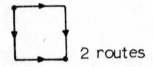

2 routes

Then look at a 2 × 2 square (numbers indicate the number of routes to any point). If there is one way to get to point *a* and two to *b*, then there must be three ways to *c*. Therefore there must be six routes to point *d*.

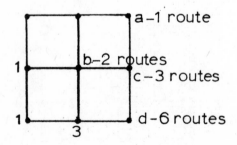

a–1 route

b–2 routes
c–3 routes

d–6 routes

Similarly, for a 3 × 3 square:

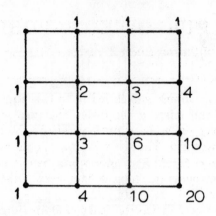

Continuing the process gives us:

Length of Edge	Number of Minimum Routes
1	2
2	6
3	20
4	70
5	252

Arthur could take a new route each day and still have plenty left over by the end of the school year!

THE PURLOINED SAPPHIRE

(Problem Starter Sheet 27, page 129)

Inspector Chang was called in to investigate the case of the missing sapphire. The gem was the centerpiece of a beautiful fountain in the middle of a courtyard. There were four rooms opening onto the courtyard, so one of four people staying in these rooms must have been responsible. But which one?

The only clue was the track of footprints left by the thief when he got his feet wet removing the sapphire. He left the path below, hoping to confuse the investigation. Chang took one look at the trail and immediately pointed at the person in room *C* as the culprit. How did she know for sure?

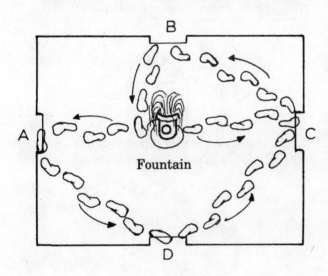

Fountain

SOLUTION: THE PURLOINED SAPPHIRE

Understand the Problem

Facts —The gem was taken from the fountain.

—The thief got wet taking it.

—The thief left a complicated trail of wet footprints from door to door, hoping to confuse the investigation.

Conditions—The thief was in a hurry so he couldn't retrace his steps. (He could walk backwards, however.)

—The thief had to end up in his own room.

—The footprints were discovered before they dried up.

Goal —By observing only the path of the crime, determine which room (*A*, *B*, *C*, or *D*) contained the culprit.

Design a Solution Strategy

Make a simple sketch of the courtyard arrangement and the footprint path. Try starting at the fountain and follow the path to see where it ends. It might be useful to design several networks, organize the results in a table, and look for a pattern.

Carry Out Plan

Using a simple diagram of the courtyard, trace several different paths.

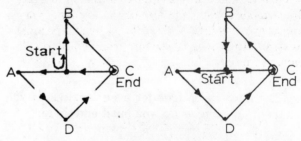

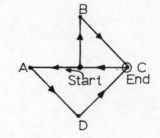

Evaluate Results

A clear pattern should be apparent. If you start at the fountain (center dot) you always end up at *C!* It might also be pointed out that only room C and the fountain are points where *three* paths come together. All other points connect only two paths. Chang learned about network problems in a topology course she had taken in college, so she knew that if you start at a point where an odd number of paths come together, you cannot end there.

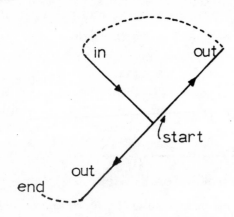

However, if you don't start at an odd vertex, you must end there.

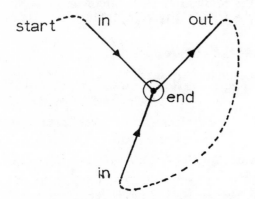

The opposite is true for even vertices. If you start at an even vertex you must end there.

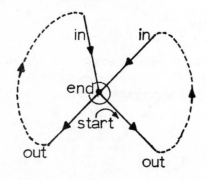

If you do not start at an even vertex, you cannot end there.

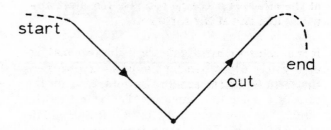

As a follow-up activity, prepare several networks and have your class determine which can be traversed without retracing any paths. See if they can discover the rule which predicts whether a figure is "traceable." Suggest that each student sketch a figure and exchange with a friend to see if it is traceable. The results make excellent bulletin boards. (See "Line'ardo DaVinci," Starter Sheet 28.)

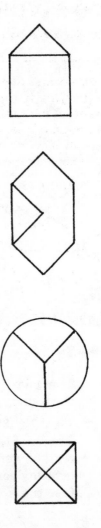

Traceable Figures. A network is traceable if it contains exactly zero or two odd vertices. If a figure has two odd vertices, start at one end and finish at the other. If it has no odd vertices, start anywhere and end at the same point.

It is also fun to investigate three-dimensional figures where edges become the paths and corners the vertices. Do the same rules apply?

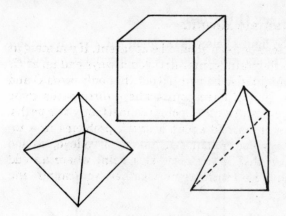

Problem and Solution 28

LINE'ARDO DaVINCI

(Problem Starter Sheet 28, page 130)

Line'ardo paints the white line down the middle of the road. He is trying to conserve fuel, so he checks out his map each morning to plan his shortest route. Can Line'ardo "line" all the roads connecting the four cities below without retracing any routes? Where should he start?

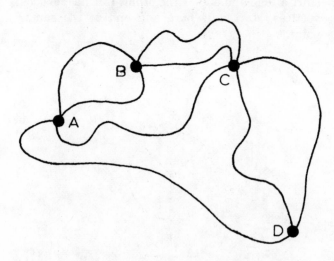

SOLUTION: LINE'ARDO DeVINCI

Understand the Problem

Facts —Four cities (*A*, *B*, *C*, and *D*) are connected by roads.

—Line'ardo must pass over every road.

Conditions—He cannot retrace his route.

—He cannot jump from one city to another.

Goal —Traverse all the routes connecting the four cities without retracing any roads.

Design a Solution Strategy

Construct a simplified drawing of the map. Experiment with various routes by tracing the simplified figure with a pencil. Arrange the results in a table.

Carry Out Plan

The figure below is an identical, though simpler, arrangement of the cities and connecting roads.

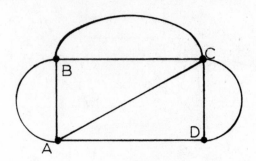

Try to trace the figure beginning at A.

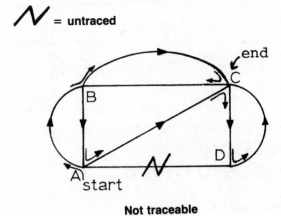

$\mathcal{N}$ = untraced

Not traceable

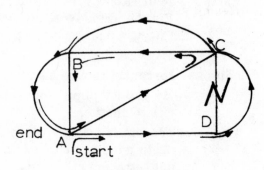

Not traceable

Conduct several experiments beginning at each city. Organize the results in a table.

Start	Traceable	End
A	No	C
A	No	A
A	No	D
B	No	A
B	No	C
C	Yes	D
C	Yes	D
D	Yes	C
D	Yes	C
D	Yes	C

Evaluate Results

Notice that complete routes are not possible when starting at A or B. Almost any route starting at C or D is traceable. If Line'ardo starts at C he will have dinner at D and vice versa. Try other networks of routes connecting 3, 4, 5 or more cities. Keep track of the even and odd vertices (number of routes coming together at a point). Can your students discover the rule for traceability? (See "The Purloined Sapphire," Starter Sheet 28.)

Traceable Figure

A network is traceable if it contains exactly zero or two odd vertices. If a figure has two odd vertices, start at one and end at the other. If it has no odd vertices, start anywhere and end at the same point.

JAILHOUSE BLUES

(Problem Starter Sheet 29, page 131)

John Turnkey, the prison warden, decided to free his prisoners for good behavior. The cells were numbered from 1 to 25. Each had a lock that opened when you turned it once and locked when it was turned again, and so on.

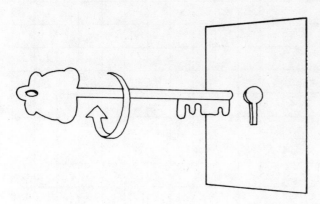

One night when the prisoners were sleeping, he quietly turned all the locks once, opening all the cells. He began to worry that he may have freed too many prisoners, so he went back and turned every second lock (2, 4, 6, 8, . . . 24) which locked half the cells. Thinking that there still might be too many prisoners freed, he gave every third lock a turn (3, 6, 9, 12, . . . 24), then every fourth lock (4, 8, 12, . . . 24), fifth (5, 10, 15, 20, 25), sixth (6, 12, 18, 24), seventh, eighth, ninth, tenth, eleventh and so on all the way to every twenty-fifth (of course he only turned one lock for every thirteenth and above).

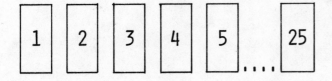

Who got out of jail in the morning?

SOLUTION: JAILHOUSE BLUES

Understand the Problem

Facts —There are twenty-five jail cells.

—The locks open with first turn, close on the next turn, and so on.

Conditions—The warden first opens all locks, then turns even numbered locks (multiples of 2), then every third lock, then multiples of 4, 5, 6, 7, 8, 9, 10, 11, all the way up to multiples of 25.

—Only one lock is turned for multiples of 13, 14, 15, . . . 25.

—Most passes through the prison open some cells and lock others.

Goal —Find which cells will be open after the above process is completed.

Design a Solution Strategy

Construct a list of cell numbers and keep track of each turn with a check mark below the appropriate cell numbers. After completing the twenty-five passes through the cells, determine the total number of turns for each cell. Look for a pattern to determine who is free.

Carry Out Plan

The following table gives a summary of twenty-five passes through the jail turning the locks as described above.

Cell Numbers

Multiple of	1	2	3	4	5	6	7	8	9	10	11	12	13	14	15	16	17	18	19	20	21	22	23	24	25
1	✓	✓	✓	✓	✓	✓	✓	✓	✓	✓	✓	✓	✓	✓	✓	✓	✓	✓	✓	✓	✓	✓	✓	✓	✓
2		✓		✓		✓		✓		✓		✓		✓		✓		✓		✓		✓		✓	
3			✓			✓			✓			✓			✓			✓			✓			✓	
4				✓				✓				✓				✓				✓				✓	
5					✓					✓					✓					✓					✓
6						✓						✓						✓						✓	
7							✓							✓							✓				
8								✓								✓								✓	
9									✓									✓							
10										✓										✓					
11											✓											✓			
12												✓												✓	
13													✓												
14														✓											
15															✓										
16																✓									
17																	✓								
18																		✓							
19																			✓						
20																				✓					
21																					✓				
22																						✓			
23																							✓		
24																								✓	
25																									✓
Total Turns	1 open	2	2	3 open	2	4	2	4	3 open	4	2	6	2	4	4	5 open	2	6	2	6	4	4	2	8	3 open

Evaluate Results

First let's observe the relationship between the number of turns and whether a lock is open or closed.

1 turn—open

2 turns—closed

3 turns—open

4 turns—closed

5 turns—open

6 turns—closed

and so on . . .

Notice that an odd number of times opens the lock, an even number closes it. Therefore the results listed in the table show that prisoners in cells 1, 4, 9, 16 and 25 will be freed.

It is interesting to note that the data collected for our jailhouse problem are identical to counting the factors for a given number. For example, 12 has six factors: 1, 2, 3, 4, 6, 12. Six is also the number of lock turns for cell 12. To find out who is freed, we simply look for numbers with an odd number of factors—the square numbers. For example, 16 has five factors: 1, 2, 4, 8, 16. Finding a functional solution (a general rule) to a problem clearly demonstrates the power of mathematics to extend solutions to more general cases. Have your class find out who would get out of jail if there were 100 cells; 1000 cells.

Problem and Solution 30

BILL YUD POOL

(Problem Starter Sheet 30, page 132)

Bill Yud was an avid pool player. He enjoyed impressing his friends with his feats of skill. He invented a new pool table that could be adjusted to almost any size and had pockets in only three of the four corners. Someone could call out any size table and old Bill would think for a minute then point to one of the pockets. Next he would place the ball in the corner with no pocket and shoot out at a 45° angle. That ball would scoot all over the table and sure enough would fall into the chosen pocket. He never missed! Can you figure out what Bill was up to? Here are a few examples.

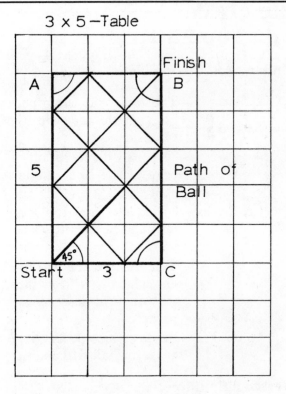

3 x 5 —Table

4 × 7 — Table

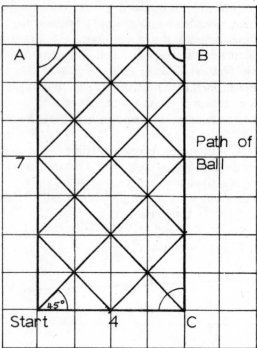

A

B

Path of Ball

7

45°

Start   4   C

Carry Out Plan

Here is the record of twelve experiments.

Ball Ends in Pocket:	A	B	C
Table (length, height)	(5, 6)	(3, 5)	(4, 7)
	(3, 4)	(5, 7)	(4, 6)
	(3, 6)	(4, 4)	(2, 3)
	(1, 2)	(2, 14)	

Initially no clear patterns become apparent. However, with a bit more experimenting we see that some games leave the same shape "track." For example, (4, 6) and (2, 3) are identical games but are different size scales.

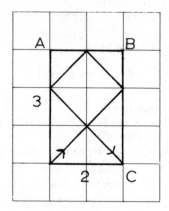

A   B

3

2   C

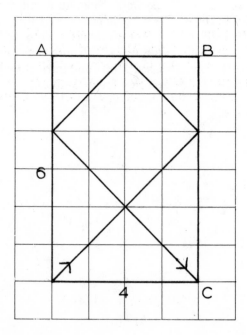

A   B

6

4   C

SOLUTION: BILL YUD POOL

Understand the Problem

Facts —The table has three pockets; length and width of table varies.

—The ball bounces off an edge at the same angle it strikes.

Conditions—Shoot out from the lower lefthand corner (no pocket) at 45°.

—You must hit the ball hard enough so it continues to roll until it reaches a pocket.

Goal —Predict which pocket (A, B, or C) the ball will end in.

Design a Solution Strategy

Using graph paper, play several "Bill Yud" games and organize the results in a table.

Therefore, if (2, 3) ends at C then (4, 6) must as well. And what about (6, 9), (8, 12) and (10, 15)? Since this whole "family" of games ends at C then it is only necessary to include the simplest (2, 3) in the table. Similarly, this is true for (1, 2) and (3, 6) in column A and (1, 7) and (2, 14) in column B.

Ball Ends in Pocket:	A	B	C
Simplest table (length, height)	(5, 6)	(3, 5)	(4, 7)
	(3, 4)	(5, 7)	(2, 3)
	(1, 2)	(1, 1)	(2, 3)
		(1, 7)	

Evaluate Results

A clear pattern now emerges. Every "table" in column A has an odd length and even height. The opposite is true for C. Tables in column B have two odd dimensions.

Test the pattern to see if it always works. Many times the rule will hold only for selected cases and will require modification after additional experimentation. In this case, the pattern holds for all "simple" tables (i.e., dimensions are relatively prime). Other tables must have their dimensions reduced (rescaled) before the prediction will be accurate.

Additional problems of interest include:

1. Which games have a track which crosses every square?
2. Can you predict how many times the ball touches the edge of the table? (Count the starting and ending points.)
3. What happens when you use triangular or circular tables?

Problem and Solution 31

FARMING A FIELD

(Problem Starter Sheet 31, page 133)

A farmer needs to know how much area his fields cover so the correct amount of seed and fertilizer can be bought. Aggie McDonald's farm has trees planted in a regular square pattern. Aggie's grandfather planted the trees years ago to help him compute the area of various shaped fields for planting.

Aggie liked to plant interesting shaped fields of corn, beans and squash. (Rectangular fields can be a bit boring to plow.) Can you use the tree pattern to help Aggie figure out these areas in unit squares? (A "unit" is the area of the small squares formed by the tree pattern.)

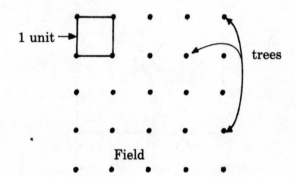

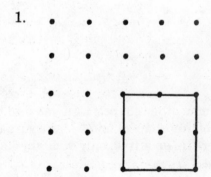

1.

2.

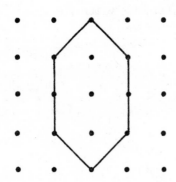

3.

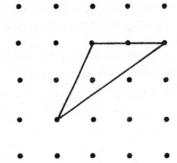

4.

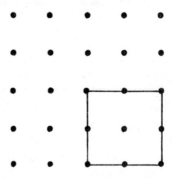

5. Try some other shapes. Can you find the area of any shaped field? (Make sure the corners lie on a tree; only straight edges please.)

SOLUTION: FARMING A FIELD

Understand the Problem

Facts —The trees form a pattern of equal squares on the field.

—A *unit square* is a square formed by four adjacent trees.

Conditions—The corners of figures must lie on a tree.

—The sides of fields must be straight lines.

Goal —Find areas of various fields in *unit squares*.

Design a Solution Strategy

Use a geoboard or dot paper as a concrete model. Break the problem into smaller parts or add something to the problem situation to ease solution.

Carry Out Plan

Place the first shape on the geoboard.

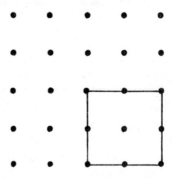

By breaking the problem up into smaller parts, the solution is clear.

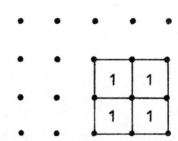

By adding a few lines to the second problem, the solution is fairly transparent.

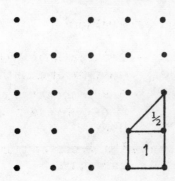

Similarly,

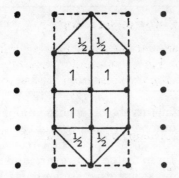

The last example cannot be easily broken into parts. Instead we fit a rectangle around the outside and see what we must "tear" off to arrive at the original figure.

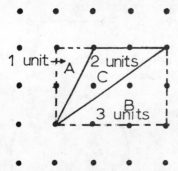

The whole rectangle has an area of six units. Triangle *A* is one half of 2 units (1 unit). Triangle *B* is one half of the whole rectangle (3 units) leaving 6 − 4 = 2 unit squares for the original triangle *C*.

Problem 5 is by far the most interesting (and most time consuming) of this set. Its solution requires gathering lots of experimental data. Tables are extremely useful in organizing the data and searching for patterns. The two key variables are:

1. The number of trees (nails) on the edge of figure (E).
2. The number of trees (nails) completely inside the field (I).

   Note. It may require considerable experimentation before these variables are identified.

The following table should be filled in as a result of your experiments.

				Inside Nails (I)				
		0	1	2	3	4	5
Edge Nails (E)	3	½	1½	2½	3½	4½	5½
	4	1	2	3	4		
	5	1½	2½	3½	4½		
	6	2	3	4	5		
	7	2½		(Area in unit squares.)			
	8						

Evaluate Results

Once patterns have been discovered, the table can be completed and tested (evaluated) for accuracy. Some students may even describe rules (functions) which describe the patterns. For example:

1. As you put one more nail inside, the area gets one unit bigger.
2. As you add one nail to the edge without changing the number inside, the area gets bigger by ½ unit.

The mathematical function which summarizes the entire relationship is:

$$\tfrac{1}{2}E + I - 1 = \text{Area}.$$

Check to see if this function always works. For example, with 6 nails on the edge and 2 inside we have:

$$(\tfrac{1}{2} \cdot 6 + 2) - 1 = (3 + 2) - 1$$
$$= 5 - 1 = 4 \text{ unit squares.}$$

Though we have evaluated each of the area problems, the discussion of problem 5 is of greatest interest since the solution seems to cover such a wide range of cases. In fact, once the general rule is thoroughly understood, previous techniques of breaking up or adding to the problem situation become unnecessary.

Additional problems of interest might include finding areas of fields on a triangular geoboard.

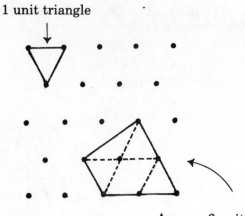

1 unit triangle

Area = 6 units

Problem and Solution 32

CLYDE THE CLASS CLOWN
(Problem Starter Sheet 32, page 134)

One day Clyde got caught putting a toad in Mrs. Purdy's purse and didn't get called on to take the lunch count to the office for days. He spent the whole weekend trying to figure out a solution for his problem. Early Monday morning he asked Mrs. Purdy if she would pick the class messenger in the following way:

> After attendance, everyone sits in a circle. Each counts off one at a time, beginning with the person to the left of the teacher (1, 2, 3, 4, . . .). Once everyone has a number, the teacher moves to the middle of the circle and begins sending children to their seats by

skipping number 1, sending number 2, skipping number 3, sending number 4, and so on until she goes around the circle completely. She doesn't stop, however, and continues skipping every other student until one is left. This lucky person gets to take the lunch count to the office. If there are ten students in the class, number 5 will be chosen.

Where should Clyde sit if there are eleven students? Twelve students? Fifteen students? Twenty students? Thirty students? Can you find a rule that works for any size class?

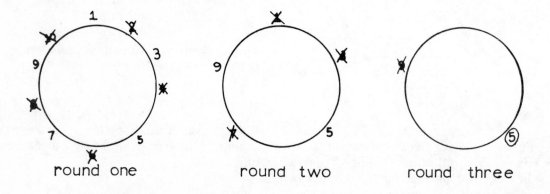

round one   round two   round three

SOLUTION: CLYDE THE CLASS CLOWN

Understand the Problem

Facts —Students count off clockwise using natural numbers (1, 2, 3, . . .). Students are eliminated by skipping every other one and continuing around the circle until only one is left. (Don't skip the number 1 position on each subsequent round unless the last person was eliminated.)

Conditions—The total number of students is known before anyone sits down.

Goal —Find where Clyde should sit if he doesn't want to be eliminated.

Design a Solution Strategy

Simplify the problem by sketching all the class sizes from one to twenty. Conduct experiments, organize the results in a table, and look for a pattern.

Carry Out Plan

The sketches below show class sizes from one to eight. The X's show the students sent to their seats. The circled position is the one remaining.

Class Size	"Lucky" Position
1	1
2	1
3	3
4	1
5	3
6	5
7	7
8	1
9	3
10	5
11	7
12	9
13	11
14	13
15	15
16	1
17	3
18	5

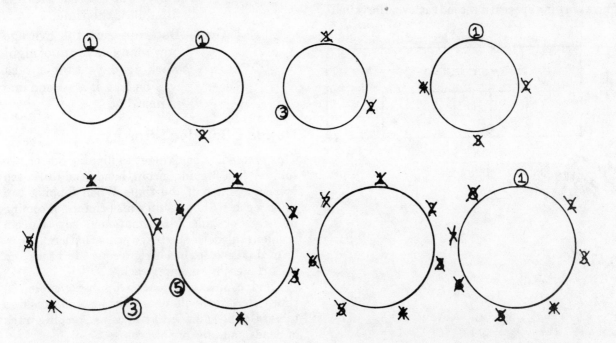

Evaluate Results

The lucky position is always an odd number. Looking at the table, notice that if the class size is one, two, four, eight or sixteen students, the lucky position is number 1. For each class size between these *key* numbers, the lucky position can be found by counting off using odd numbers. For example, if there are twenty-four students, the *largest* key number is 16. For each number (16 through 24), count off odd numbers until you reach 24: 1 (16), 3 (17), 5 (18), 7 (19), 9 (20), 11 (21), 13 (22), 15 (23), 17 (24). For twenty-four students the lucky position is number 17.

If your class is bigger than thirty-one students (and whose isn't these days?), you will find the next key number is 32 (lucky position number 1). Notice that the key numbers seem to grow by a doubling process.

This sequence is also known as the "powers of two": 2^0, 2^1, 2^2, ... What is the next key number after 32? (See "Stack the Deck," page 66, for a similar problem.)

Problem and Solution 33

THE BICYCLE DILEMMA

(Problem Starter Sheet 33, page 135)

Cary rode her bicycle to the pet store after school every day to help clean the bird cages. There was only one bike rack near the store and Cary noticed it was full about half the time. She tried to convince the shop owner to put in one more rack so she wouldn't have to worry about losing her bike while she was working.

With one bike rack Cary can lock her bike four out of eight times she works. On the average, how many out of every eight working days should she find a parking space if a second rack was installed?

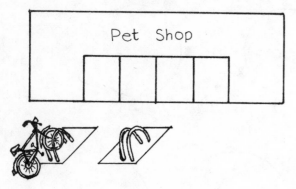

SOLUTION: THE BICYCLE DILEMMA

Understand the Problem

Facts—One bike rack is used half the time.

Conditions—Assume there are enough bicycles so that each rack is filled half the time.

Goal—Determine on the average how many days out of eight working days that a rack will be free if a second one is installed.

Design a Solution Strategy

This problem is equivalent to flipping one or two coins. When flipping a coin, heads and tails each appear about half the time. When flipping two coins, each still has a fifty-fifty chance of coming up heads or tails. Mathematicians say the coin problem "models" the bike rack situation.

In this case, let heads represent a full rack and tails represent an empty rack.

Conduct an experiment by flipping one coin 100 times. Record the number of heads and tails in a table. Do the same with two coins, keeping track of heads and tails of both coins.

Carry Out Plan

The table below shows a record of 100 flips of a single coin:

One Coin Experiment

Heads	Tails
卌	卌
卌	卌
卌	卌
卌	卌
卌	卌
卌	卌
卌	卌
卌	卌
卌	卌
1111	卌 1
49	51

For two coins there are three possible outcomes:

Two Coin Experiment

Both Heads	Both Tails	Heads and Tails
卌 卌	卌 卌	卌 卌
卌 卌	卌 卌	卌 卌
卌 1	卌	卌 卌
		卌 卌
		卌 1111
26	25	49

Evaluate Results

Notice that the results in the first experiment confirm our expectations that we should get heads about half the time. This result is analogous to the one-rack situation.

The results using two coins are more interesting. If tails represents a vacant bike rack, either column two or three above will offer Cary security. Only the "both heads" column leaves no space available to lock her bike. Out of 100 flips of two coins, 74 coins (about three-fourths) provide at least one tail (open bike rack). On the average, then, Cary should find an open rack approximately three-fourths of the time, or six out of eight days.

Without doing an experiment of this type, it is easy to assume that since there are enough bicycles around to keep all the bike racks full about half the time, the chances of finding a free rack should remain the same—about one-half or 50 percent. The coin experiment exposes this false assumption.

Your students might be interested in investigating the situation with three, four or five bike racks available. Just use a like number of coins and start flipping. A word of caution, however. This problem quickly gets as messy as a bird cage.

BIBLIOGRAPHY

Arithmetic Teacher. (Problem Solving Issue), Volume 25, February 1978.

BURNS, MARILYN. *The Book of Think*. New York: Little Brown and Company, 1978.

———. *I Hate Math*. New York: Little Brown and Company, 1977.

———. *The Good Time Math Event Book*. Palo Alto, CA: Creative Publications, 1977.

DUDENEY, HENRY E. *The Canterbury Puzzles*. New York: Dover Publications Inc., 1958.

GARDNER, MARTIN. *Mathematical Puzzles and Diversions*. New York: Dover Publications Inc., 1966.

———. *Mathematics, Magic and Mystery*. New York: Dover Publications Inc., 1956.

GREENES, CAROL, RITA SPUNGIN AND JUSTINE M. DOMBROWSKI. *Problem-Mathics: Mathematical Challenge Problems with Solution Strategies*. Palo Alto, CA: Creative Publications, 1977.

JACOBS, HAROLD R. *Mathematics: A Human Endeavor*. San Francisco: W. H. Freeman and Company, 1970.

KEYSER, TAMARA AND RANDALL SOUVINEY. *Measurement and The Child's Environment*. Santa Monica, CA: Goodyear Publishing Company, 1980.

LOYD, SAM. *Mathematical Puzzles of Sam Loyd*. 2 vols. (Edited by Martin Gardner.) New York: Dover Publications Inc., 1952.

POLYA, GEORGE. *Mathematical Discovery: On Understanding, Learning and Teaching Problem Solving*. 2 vols. New York: John Wiley and Sons, 1962.

———. *How to Solve It*. Princeton: Princeton University Press, 1957.

SEYMOUR, DALE, VERDA HOLMBERG AND MARY LAYCOCK. *Aftermath*. Palo Alto, CA: Creative Publications, 1975.

SEYMOUR, DALE AND MARGARET SHEDD. *Finite Differences: A Problem Technique*. Palo Alto, CA: Creative Publications, 1973.

SILVERSTEIN, SHEL. *Where The Sidewalk Ends*. New York: Harper and Row, 1974.

SOUVINEY, RANDALL. "Math Problems—Life Problems," *Teacher Magazine*. February 1979.

———. "Recreational Mathematics," *Learning Magazine*. May 1977.

SOUVINEY, RANDALL, TAMARA KEYSER AND ALAN SARVER. *Mathmatters: Developing Computational Skills With Developmental Activity Sequences*. Santa Monica, CA: Goodyear Publishing Company, 1978.

WERTHEIMER, MAX. *Productive Thinking*. New York: Harper & Row, 1959.

WIRTZ, ROBERTS. *Banking on Problem Solving*. Washington, D.C.: Curriculum Development Associates, 1976.

Reproducible Problem Starter Sheets

Name _____

Date _____

TOOTH TRUTHS

Which class in your school is missing the most teeth?

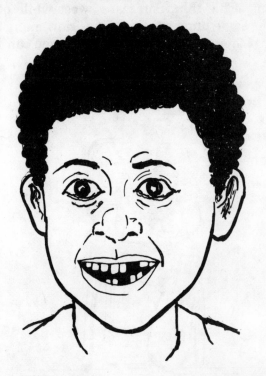

Hint: Fill in the table to help you find out:

Teacher	Grade	Missing Teeth

Name _____

Date _____

_____

FRUIT FACTS

_____

Oranges are a famous fruit first found in China. They come in many sizes and colors. Some have thick skins, some thin. Some are sweet while others are bitter. Do all oranges have the same number of sections? How many seeds are in an orange? Does it matter if they are big or small? See if you can find out.

Hint: Next time you're at the grocery store, talk with the grocer about the different types of oranges. Peel one and count the seeds and sections. Write your answer on a piece of paper and compare it with your friend's.

Seeds	Sections

Name _____

Date _____

MYSTERY MASSES

You need:

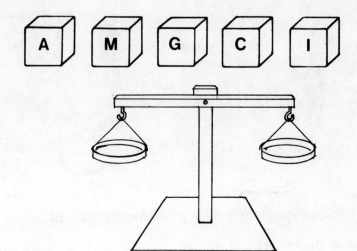

and

Put the boxes in order from lightest to heaviest. Write the *mystery word* the boxes spell:

_____ _____ _____ _____ _____

light   heavy

 Hint: Use the ⚖ to help you compare the mystery masses.

Name _____

Date _____

APPLE SHARING

You will need:

you

two friends

one apple

Share the apple so that you and your two friends get the same amount.

How many seeds are in the apple?
Do all apples have the same number of seeds?

Apple Name	Number of Seeds
1.	
2.	
3.	

Put the seeds in the sun for a few days. Plant them and see what happens.

Hint: Take turns cutting the apple. The last person to cut chooses last. Go to the supermarket and talk to the grocer about apples.

Name _____

Date _____

CLAY BOATS

You need:

clay

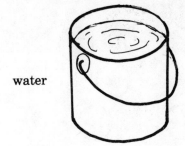
water

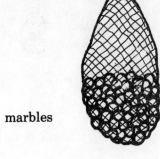
marbles

Can you make a clay boat that floats?
Try it.
See how many marbles it will carry.

Hint: Pinch the walls very thin and plug any holes.

Name _____

Date _____

CHANGING CHANGE

How many ways could you make change for 16¢?
You need:

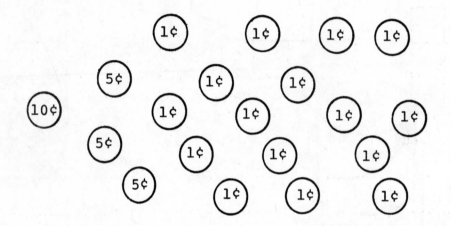

💡 **Hint:** Fill in the table below. Count the *different* ways to make change for 16¢.

	10¢	5¢	1¢	
1	1 dime	1 nickel	1 penny	= 16¢
2				= 16¢
3				= 16¢
4				= 16¢
5				= 16¢
6				= 16¢
7				= 16¢
8				= 16¢

Name _____

Date _____

CANDY BARS

Here are some whole candy bars:

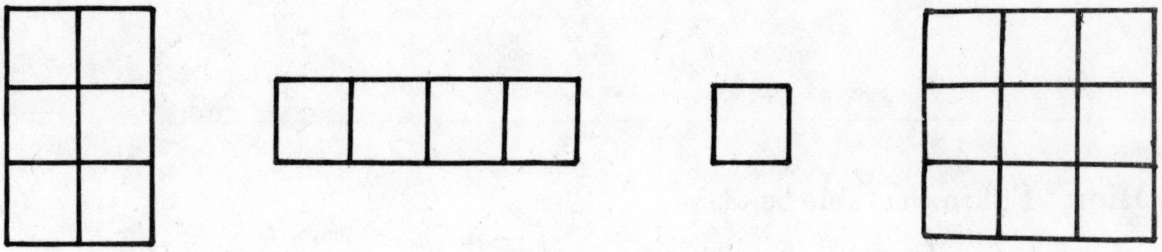

Here are some candy bars with bites out of them:

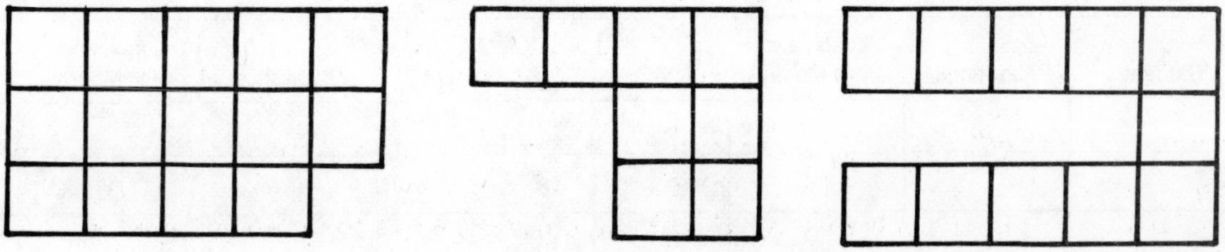

No candy bar can have more than nine units on an edge:

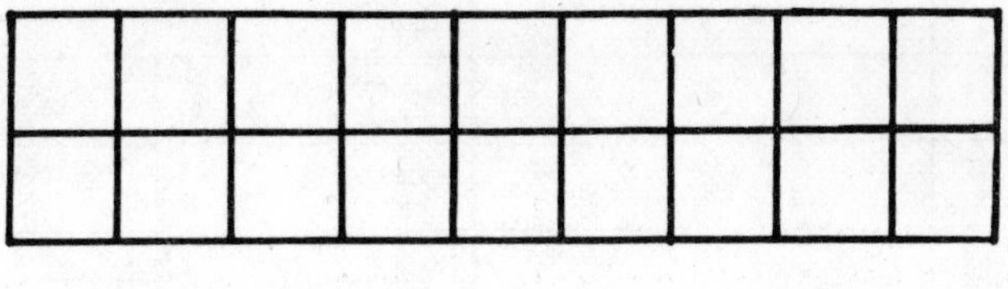

How many different candy bars can you make?

> **Hint:** Using squared paper, cut out as many different candy bars as you can.

Remember: 3 [2×3 grid figure] 2   is the same as: 2 [3×2 grid figure] 3

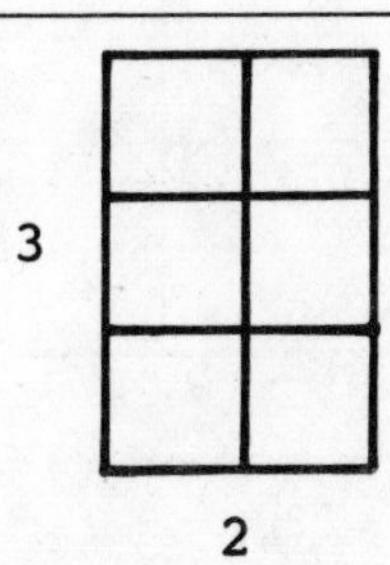

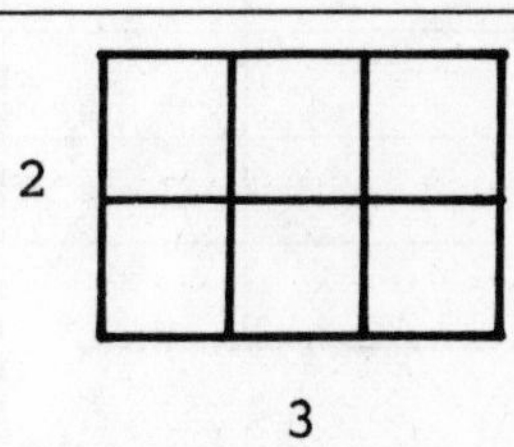

Name _____

Date _____

CLASS ALLOWANCE

How much money does your class spend in a year? To find out you need:

> 💡 **Hint:** Fill in the table below.

Class Income for One Week

Student	Allowance	Lunch and Milk Money	Total	Student	Allowance	Lunch and Milk Money	Total
1.				17.			
2.				18.			
3.				19.			
4.				20.			
5.				21.			
6.				22.			
7.				23.			
8.				24.			
9.				25.			
10.				26.			
11.				27.			
12.				28.			
13.				29.			
14.				30.			
15.				31.			
16.				32.			
				Total For One Week			
				For One Year ($\times$ 52)			

Name _____

Date _____

PENCIL SURVIVAL

How long does a pencil last in your class? To find out you will need:

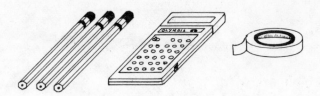

Hint: Before a new pencil is passed out, put a small piece of tape around the top. Write the date it is first sharpened. When it is used up, fill in the table below:

Pencil Life Span

	Date First Sharpened	Date Used Up	Number of School Days Used
1.			
2.			
3.			
4.			
5.			
6.			
7.			
8.			
9.			
10.			
		Total	

Use a calculator to find the average. Divide the total days by the number of pencils. Average: _____ .

Name _____

Date _____

T.V. HOURS

How much television do you watch in one year? To find out you need:

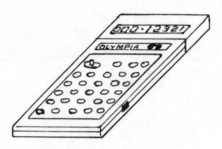

Hint: For a week fill in your T.V. time below. Use a calculator to help you find your total number of T.V. hours in one year.

Day	T.V. Hours
Monday	
Tuesday	
Wednesday	
Thursday	
Friday	
Saturday	
Sunday	
Total For Week	
Total For Year (× 52)	

Name _____

Date _____

HOT LUNCH

Which school lunch does your class like best? To find out you need:

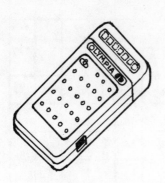

School Lunch Menu - May

Mon	Tues	Wed	Thur	Fri

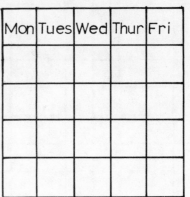

Hint: Fill in the table with the number of buyers and brownbaggers. Use your calculator to help you find which foods are the most popular.

Week	Monday	Tuesday	Wednesday	Thursday	Friday
1.	Menu _____ Buy _____ Bring _____ Total _____	Menu _____ Buy _____ Bring _____ Total _____	Menu _____ Buy _____ Bring _____ Total _____	Menu _____ Buy _____ Bring _____ Total _____	Menu _____ Buy _____ Bring _____ Total _____
2.	Menu _____ Buy _____ Bring _____ Total _____	Menu _____ Buy _____ Bring _____ Total _____	Menu _____ Buy _____ Bring _____ Total _____	Menu _____ Buy _____ Bring _____ Total _____	Menu _____ Buy _____ Bring _____ Total _____
3.	Menu _____ Buy _____ Bring _____ Total _____	Menu _____ Buy _____ Bring _____ Total _____	Menu _____ Buy _____ Bring _____ Total _____	Menu _____ Buy _____ Bring _____ Total _____	Menu _____ Buy _____ Bring _____ Total _____
4.	Menu _____ Buy _____ Bring _____ Total _____	Menu _____ Buy _____ Bring _____ Total _____	Menu _____ Buy _____ Bring _____ Total _____	Menu _____ Buy _____ Bring _____ Total _____	Menu _____ Buy _____ Bring _____ Total _____

Name _____

Date _____

FOLDING BOXES

Which of these twelve figures will fold into an open-end box? Fold only on dotted lines.

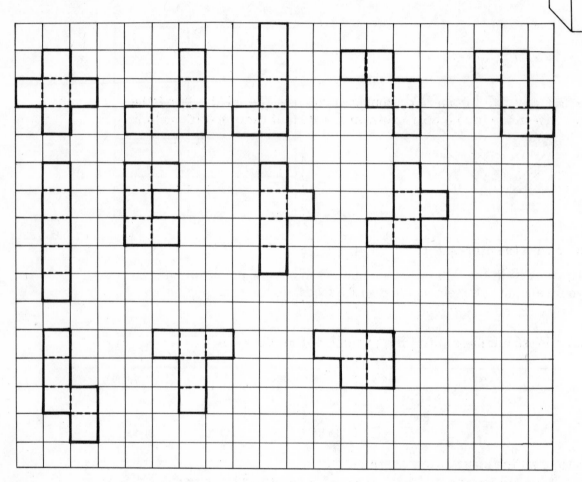

> **Hint:** Cut out these figures and try to fold them into a box. You might also try cutting off the top of several small milk cartons and see which of the above shapes you can make by cutting along the edges. Remember, the figure must be in one piece.

Name _____

Date _____

WHAT'S THE DIFFERENCE?

Pick any four numbers and write them in a square, as below.

4   8

2   1

Next, connect any two numbers without going across the middle. Find the difference between the two number values and write it at the center of the line.

Do the same with the other pairs.

Now connect these numbers with lines and find their differences.

This time all the answers are the same.
Will this always happen for any four starting numbers?
Will you always end up with 2 for a final answer?
What happens if you start with bigger numbers?
This problem needed three steps to get to a common difference. Can you find four numbers that need four steps? Five steps? Six steps?

 Hint: Try many combinations of four numbers. Keep a record of the original four numbers, the number of differences, and the final answer.

Name _____

Date _____

GOLD DIGGERS

Digger Jenkins was a gold assayer who flew all over Alaska in a rickety little plane weighing ore for eager prospectors. His job was to weigh samples very accurately, but he also had to be careful not to overload his tiny plane with equipment. To measure, he packed only a balance and three mass pieces—1 gram, 3 gram and 9 gram weights. For example, he could weigh a 4-gram sample of gold ore like this:

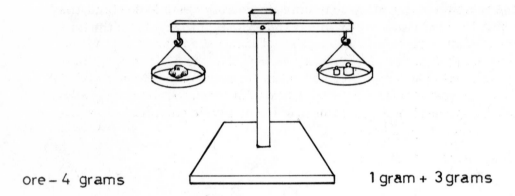

ore – 4 grams   1 gram + 3 grams

Digger claimed he could weigh any amount of ore from 1 to 13 grams. (No fractions, of course.) Is Digger right?

Hint: Find a pan balance and the three mass pieces, conduct several experiments and organize the results in a table. Remember, the mass pieces can go on either pan.

Name _____

Date _____

THE GREAT DIVIDE

Otto Levique and his family were taking a trip across Canada by car. When they came to the Rocky Mountains, his daughter, Michelle, who had been studying geography in school, explained that they would soon cross the Great Divide—an imaginary line running lengthwise along the highest points of a mountain range. Rain falling to the east of this line ends up in the Atlantic Ocean and to the west, in the Pacific Ocean. It was an exciting moment when they crossed the "roof of the continent," but they were all surprised when they crossed the imaginary line more than once. Look at the map to see how this could happen.

Michelle kept a record of the number of times they crossed the Great Divide. She thought it was odd that they crossed the line five times on their route from Edmonton to Vancouver and seven times on their return, making a total of twelve crossings for the round trip. Will every round trip through the mountains always have an even number of Great Divide crossings? Help the Leviques with their auto-dilemma.

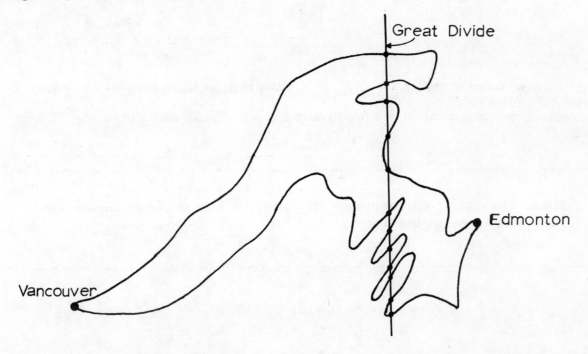

Hint: Draw a map of an imaginary Great Divide. Do several experiments, organize the results in a table, and look for patterns.

Name _____

Date _____

STACK THE DECK

Here is an interesting card trick to try with your friends. Write each letter of your name on separate, identical cards. Form them into a deck with the faces down and shuffle the deck. Slip the top card under the deck, still face down. Deal the second card face up on the table. Slip the third card under the deck and deal the next card face up next to the first. Continue this process until all the cards form a line on the table.

You would be lucky indeed if the cards spelled a word. However, can you find a way to stack the deck so that when you deal out the cards as above, it spells your name?

Slip one card under deck.   **Deal next card face up.**

If you can figure out a solution, it's fun to surprise your friends using their names.

 Hint: Try starting with your name spelled on the table and follow the steps backwards to arrange the deck.

Name _____

Date _____

FOUR ACES

This simple card trick sounds complicated but it is actually very easy to do.

1. Using an ordinary deck of cards cut the cards into four roughly equal piles and lay them out next to each other in front of you.

2. Pick up the pile that came from the bottom of the deck (pile 4), and deal three cards face down on the table in the same spot where the pile was.

3. Deal one card from pile 4 face down on top of each of the other three decks and place the pile back where it came from, on top of the three cards.

4. Repeat the process with the other three piles, ending with the pile that was on top of the original deck (pile 1).

5. Turning over the top card on each pile gives a surprising result—4 aces!

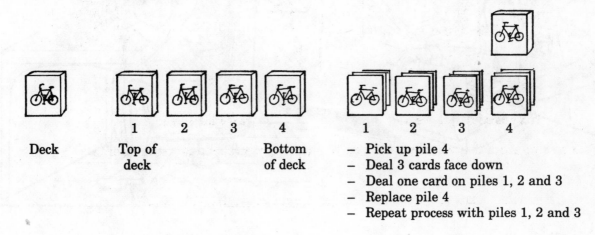

Deck   Top of deck (1)   2   3   Bottom of deck (4)

1   2   3   4
- Pick up pile 4
- Deal 3 cards face down
- Deal one card on piles 1, 2 and 3
- Replace pile 4
- Repeat process with piles 1, 2 and 3

Can you figure out how the trick works?

 Hint: Work the problem backwards and see how to stack the deck with the four aces.

119

Name _____

Date _____

STACK 'EM HIGH

Suzanne Megapenny is very rich. She got a bit bored one day and told her banker to immediately deliver one million new one dollar bills to her house. She sat in her living room and began to stack the bills on top of each other in a single column. How high will the stack be?

Hint: Find how many dollars (pieces of paper) it takes to make a pile 1 centimeter thick. Use your calculator to find the height of a million.

Name _____

Date _____

COUNT ON

One rainy afternoon Tara couldn't find anyone to play with, so she decided to count to a billion. Can you find out about how long it would take Tara to finish? One hour? Two hours? All day?

How old are you in seconds?

Hint: Figure it takes about one second to say one number and use your calculator to help you crunch the big numbers.

Name _____

Date _____

GRAINS OF RICE

How many grains of rice are in a bag of rice? One hundred grains? One thousand grains? One million grains? To find out you need

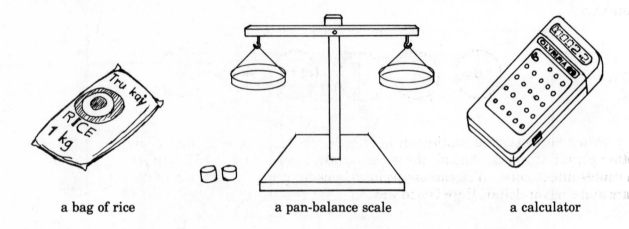

a bag of rice   a pan-balance scale   a calculator

Hint: Measure out one small cup of rice. Count the grains in the cup. Use the pan balance and calculator to help find the total number of grains in the bag.

Name _____

Date _____

MONEY MATTERS

One day, Rosa decided to play a trick on her brother, Aaron. She said, "I have 21¢ in my pocket. If you can tell me all the possible combinations of pennies, nickels and dimes which make up 21¢, I'll buy you an ice cream cone." Here is one way:

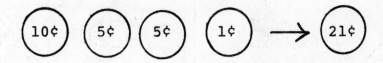

After Aaron started making his list Rosa said, "I just found a dollar in my other pocket. If you can find all the ways to make change for $1.21 I'll buy you a double-dipper cone." You can use pennies, nickels, dimes, quarters, half dollars and a silver dollar. Here is one way:

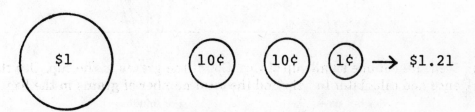

Hint: Make a list of all the ways to make change for 21¢ and $1.21. Try to follow a regular pattern so you don't skip any answers.

Name _____

Date _____

ICE-CREAM EXPERT

Bud was an expert ice-cream eater. He could name any flavor blindfolded. When he bought an ice-cream cone not only did he choose the flavors carefully, but he had to have them stacked on the cone in the right order. Strawberry on top with vanilla on the bottom was for hot days. Vanilla on top and strawberry on the bottom helped him to think better.

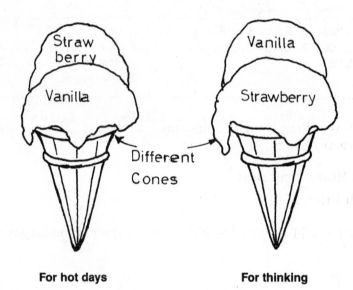

For hot days   **For thinking**

There are only two ways of building a cone with two flavors. (You must use both flavors.) How many different cones could Bud order with three flavors? Four flavors? Five flavors?

Hint: Make a list of all possible cones. Start with one flavor, then two and so on. Try to follow a pattern so you won't skip any. Using different colored blocks as flavors may help you keep track of the different cones.

Name _____

Date _____

HAMBURGER HEAVEN

Here is the menu for the local hamburger hangout.

Hamburger Heaven

Menu		
Burgers	*Fries 'n Rings*	*Drinks*
1. Boring Burger ....30¢	1. French Fries ....45¢	1. Orange ....30¢
2. Kiloburger ....75¢	2. Onion Rings ....65¢	2. Coke ....30¢
3. Fat Mac $1.50		3. Root Beer ....30¢
		4. Milk ....55¢

If you could pick one item from each column, how many different meals could you make? Here are two different meals:

1. Fat Mac, Onion Rings, Root Beer
2. Fat Mac, French Fries, Milk

How many meals would be possible if one more type of hamburger was added to the menu?

Hint: Make a list of meals. Try to follow a regular pattern so you won't miss any combinations.

Name _____

Date _____

POPCORN TRUTH

Companies are always advertising that their product is better than the rest. "Our toothpaste makes your teeth whiter"; "Kids eat more Corn Puffies than any other cereal." Ever wonder if the commercials are true? Here is an ad for you to test out for yourself.

You pay a little more, but our popcorn leaves fewer unpopped kernels, so it's a better buy.

Go to the store and buy the same size bag of the *most* expensive and *least* expensive popcorn. Do an experiment to find out if the expensive popcorn is actually a better buy.

 Hint: Pop equal amounts and compare the results to the purchase price. Use a calculator to help with the arithmetic.

Name _____

Date _____

COW THOUGHTS

Pico Steerman, a well-known rancher, invented a new style corral for his cattle. By driving a herd of steers through gate *A*, the cow-doctor could check them one at a time for disease at station *B*.

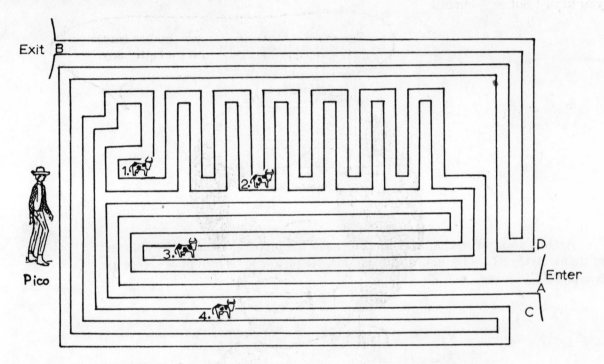

Sometimes a stray cow wanders into the maze through the opening at *C* or *D*, and though it appears to be trapped in the corral, it is actually free. Help Pico, who is standing outside the corral, figure out a way to quickly determine which steers are inside the corral and which are free to roam the range. Can you figure out a method that will always work, regardless of the position of the cow or how complex the maze? Remember, Pico can't look down on the corral, as shown in the picture above.

Hint: Try making a very simple corral which looks like an ordinary circle and figure out a simple way to show that a cow is inside. Think about what must be true for a cow to be really trapped. If you're outside, how many fences are between you and the cow? Make the corral more and more complicated; keep a record of your results and look for patterns. Do the same with the cow outside.

Name _____

Date _____

CLASSROOM MANEUVERS

Mr. Nitpicker's classroom is organized in five neat rows with five desks in each row. The desks are separated so you can walk in front and behind, as well as between them.

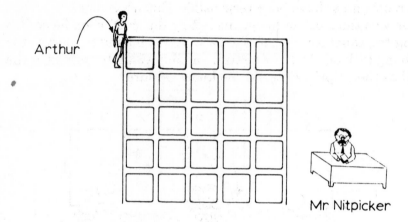

Arthur and the teacher are standing as in the picture. What is the shortest route for Arthur to walk in order to ask Mr. Nitpicker for a hall pass? Here are two possible routes:

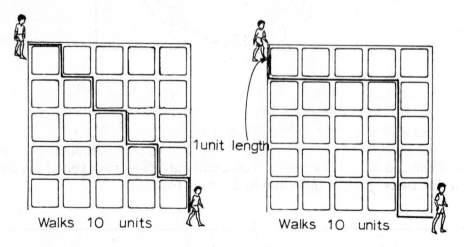

1 unit length

Walks 10 units   Walks 10 units

Hint: Find some squared paper and mark off several five-unit squares. Using this simple sketch (model), trace several routes and count the number of units Arthur has to walk.

Name _____

Date _____

THE PURLOINED SAPPHIRE

Inspector Chang was called in to investigate the case of the missing sapphire. The gem was the centerpiece of a beautiful fountain in the middle of a court-yard. There were four rooms opening onto the courtyard, so one of four people staying in these rooms must have been responsible. But which one?

   The only clue was the track of footprints left by the thief when he got his feet wet removing the sapphire. He left the path below, hoping to confuse the investigation. Chang took one look at the trail and immediately pointed at the person in room *C* as the culprit. How did she know for sure?

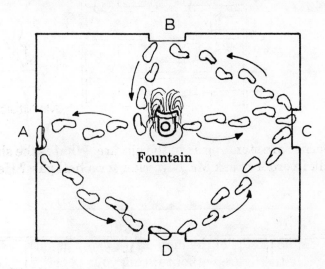

Fountain

 Hint: Make a simple sketch of the culprit's path and try tracing it without lifting your pencil or going over a line twice. Design other simple networks like those below and see if they can be traced without lifting your pencil or going over a line twice. Keep a table and look for a pattern.

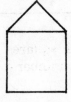 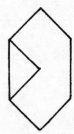 

Name _____

Date _____

LINE'ARDO DaVINCI

Line'ardo paints the white line down the middle of the road. He is trying to conserve fuel, so he checks out his map each morning to plan his shortest route. Can Line'ardo "line" all the roads connecting the four cities below without retracing any routes? Where should he start?

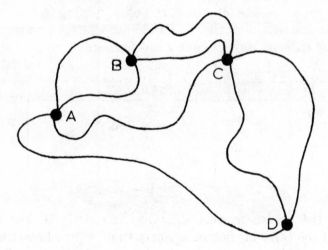

 Hint: Make a simple sketch of the map above using as many straight lines as possible. Try tracing the figure without lifting your pencil or retracing any routes. It may be helpful to experiment first with *very* simple figures, record the results and look for patterns.

Name _____

Date _____

JAILHOUSE BLUES

John Turnkey, the prison warden, decided to free his prisoners for good behavior. The cells were numbered from 1 to 25. Each had a lock that opened when you turned it once and locked when it was turned again, and so on.

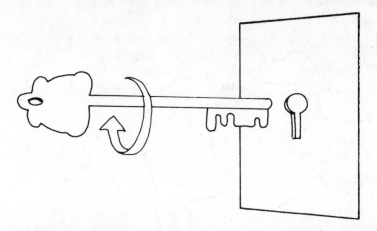

—First turn—open
—Second turn—closed
—Third turn—open
And so on . . .

One night when the prisoners were sleeping, he quietly turned all the locks once, opening all the cells. He began to worry that he may have freed too many prisoners so he went back and turned every second lock (2, 4, 6, 8, . . . 24) which locked half the cells. Thinking that there still might be too many prisoners freed, he gave every third lock a turn (3, 6, 9, 12, . . . 24), then every fourth lock (4, 8, 12, . . . 24), fifth (5, 10, 15, 20, 25), sixth (6, 12, 18, 24), seventh, eighth, ninth, tenth, eleventh and so on all the way to the every twenty-fifth (of course, he only turned one lock for every thirteenth and above).

Who got out of jail in the morning?

 Hint: Make a list of cells numbered 1 to 25. Keep track of the turns for each; look for a pattern.

Name _____

Date _____

BILL YUD POOL

Bill Yud was an avid pool player. He enjoyed impressing his friends with his feats of skill. He invented a new pool table that could be adjusted to almost any size and had pockets in only three of the four corners. Someone could call out any size table and old Bill would think for a minute then point to one of the pockets. Next he would place the ball in the corner with no pocket and shoot out at a 45° angle. That ball would scoot all over the table and sure enough would fall into the chosen pocket. He never missed! Can you figure out what Bill was up to? Here are a few examples.

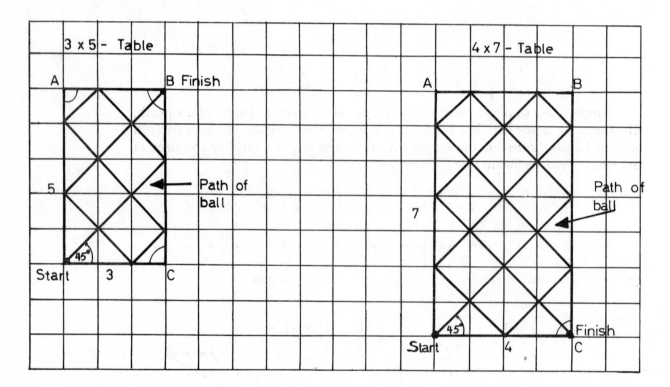

 Hint: Find some 1 cm graph paper and play several games on different size "Bill Yud" tables. Organize the data in a table and look for patterns.

Name _____

Date _____

FARMING A FIELD

A farmer needs to know how much area his fields cover so the correct amount of seed and fertilizer can be bought. Aggie McDonald's farm has trees planted in a regular square pattern. Aggie's grandfather planted the trees years ago to help him compute the area of various shaped fields for planting.

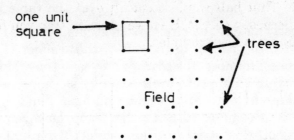

Aggie liked to plant interesting shaped fields of corn, beans and squash. (Rectangular fields can be a bit boring to plow.) Can you use the tree pattern to help Aggie figure out these areas in unit squares? (A "unit" is the area of the small squares formed by the tree pattern.)

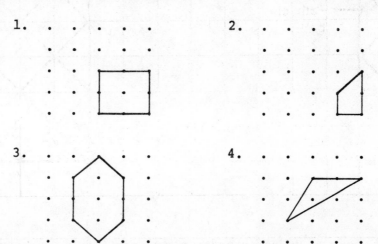

5. Try some other shapes. Can you find the area of any shaped field? (Make sure the corners lie on a tree; only straight edges please.)

 Hint: You might try using a geoboard to help "field" these problems.

Name _____

Date _____

CLYDE THE CLASS CLOWN

One day Clyde got caught putting a toad in Mrs. Purdy's purse and didn't get called on to take the lunch count to the office for days. He spent the whole weekend trying to figure out a solution for his problem. Early Monday morning he asked Mrs. Purdy if she would pick the class messenger in the following way:

> After attendance, everyone sits in a circle. Each student counts off one at a time, beginning with the person to the left of the teacher (1, 2, 3, 4, . . .). Once everyone has a number, the teacher moves to the middle of the circle and begins sending children to their seats by skipping number 1, sending number 2, skipping number 3, sending number 4 and so on until she goes around the circle completely. She doesn't stop, however, and continues skipping every other student until one is left. This lucky person gets to take the lunch count to the office. If there are ten students in the class, number 5 will be chosen.

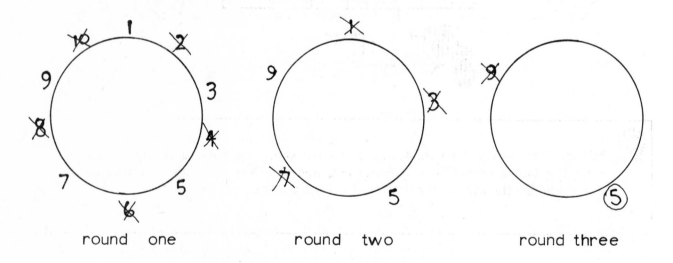

round one   round two   round three

Where should Clyde sit if there are eleven students? Twelve students? Fifteen students? Twenty students? Twenty-five students? Thirty students? Can you find a rule that works for any size class?

 Hint: Make sketches of different size class circles and organize the results in a table. Look for patterns.

Name _____

Date _____

THE BICYCLE DILEMMA

Cary rode her bicycle to the pet store after school every day to help clean the bird cages. There was only one bike rack near the store and Cary noticed it was full about half the time. She tried to convince the shop owner to put in one more rack so she wouldn't have to worry about losing her bike while she was working.

   With one bike rack Cary can lock her bike when she works four out of eight times. On the average, how many out of every eight working days should she find a parking space if a second rack was installed?

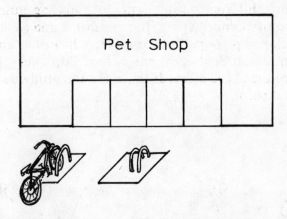

 Hints: The problem is similar to flipping two coins. Let heads represent a full rack, and tails an empty one. Flip one coin and keep a record of heads and tails in a table. Do the same with two coins. Look for a pattern.

Name _____

Date _____

_____

_____

Describe your favorite problem here and share it with your class.